Stand Up!

A Message to the Black Man

A Message of Hope and a Call to Action

Alan D. Benson, MBA, MPA

MHB Publishing
101 North 7th Street
Louisville, KY 40202
www.alandbenson.com
Email: alan@alandbenson.com

DEDICATION

I dedicate this book to my mother, Marthella H. Benson. Your love, encouragement, and level of accountability have made me the man I am today. For that, your teachings shall continue to guide my thoughts in my daily journey. Because of you, I am!

ACKNOWLEDGMENT

I would like to thank God for giving me the insight, spirit, drive, and knowledge to write this book. God has been mighty good to me. I first wrestled with writing this book, but it kept coming back in my spirit, so I saw it as a calling to move on this endeavor. I came up with the title *Stand Up! A Message to the Black Man* as a clarion call for the Black man to get focused, forge ahead in life, and live the life God intended for you to live. I know it is hard to face some of the decisions you made in the past, but I do know through God, having faith, and focusing on your journey, you can achieve anything.

Writing this book involved a great deal of self-reflection, conversation, research, surveying, and interviews with several people. I would like to thank all the men and women who participated in the surveys. They contributed significantly to shaping a perspective of why we, as Black men, interact in our relationships the way we do and how we view society. I also would like to thank the gentlemen who allowed me to interview them. From the deepest of my heart, I want to thank Gary Thompson, Maurice Aker, Kevin Haggard Sr., Ramon Thomas, Danny Johnson, Chris Goodwin, Kevin Brown, William Hudson, Robert Graves Jr., Carl Lomax, Donnie Adkins, and Donatus Weobong. These men come from various backgrounds, were raised in different eras, and grew up under various circumstances that shaped who they are today. The interviews highlight how each man carved out his path to success. While this book speaks specifically to Black men, several women contributed, and I would like to thank Susan, Ann, Pam, and Stephanie! I am most thankful for my editor, Yvonne Jackson; my associate editor, Chris Goodwin; and my creative designer, Audra Gray.

I give a great deal of gratitude to my mother, Marthella H. Benson, who not only gave me life, but the nurturance and push for me to be the best man I can be. Mom's moral fabric was wrapped around the teachings of God. She raised me according to HIS WORD and dared me always to do right. She never gave up on me, even when I felt like giving up on myself. She pushed me, and for that I am forever grateful and assured that she lives on in my heart. I love you, Mom!

Table of Contents

PREFACE

Stand up! A Message to the Black Man is a clarion call for all Black men, despite what is going on in our lives, to stand up and climb to a higher calling in our lives and become the best men we can be. While racism and unjust policies may have slowed our progress, they have not shaken our spirit or resolve. We have a rich history of serving and leading our communities. We fought in the Civil War as the 54th Massachusetts Infantry Regiment, flew in World War II as the Tuskegee Airmen, stimulated economies as mayors, made outstanding contributions as sports figures, acquired billion-dollar companies, and became President of the United States. These accomplishments opened doors for us, but we must not lose sight that our work is not complete. It is time for us to lift our torches higher and march to higher grounds for ourselves and the community.

It is unfortunate that racism still exists in the United States and comes in different forms. To combat and change it requires a changing of the hearts and actions of men. While we cannot control the hearts of men, we can control our own actions, and that is why I wrote this book—for us as Black men to look at our inner selves, and define who we are and how we operate, and make necessary adjustments. As Black men we must act now, because the global community is becoming more complex and more competitive. If we do not work together, we will continue to be left behind and surrender to either being impoverished or serving others, to our own neglect. The action steps we as Black men must take are the following:

- Keep God in our lives and rely on Him for guidance.

- Lead and protect our families and children.

- Take the lead in the community and give service.

- Be our brother's keeper through mentorship and support.

- Create an economic foundation for ourselves and the community.

- Form strategic alliances to create a robust economic foundation.

- Become more involved in the political process.

It is a must that we create our destiny as Black Men, because now is the time. Throughout history, we saw various cultures capitalize on systems and policies that helped to sustain them and their communities. That was so because they were in the ruling class, as they enslaved and lynched many of our forefathers. Moreover, Black Americans were discriminated against through Jim Crow laws and policies from having any form of economic progress, that is, both overt and systemic racism. While systemic racism exists, we as Black Americans must navigate through the maze of discrimination and fight for justice and equality. We must continue to push forward, and quitting is not an option. Our communities need our leadership, wisdom, intellectual capital, and inherent strength to mentor and cultivate our children. We must respect ourselves and trust one another to build strategic alliances. This is of the utmost importance because our ability to work together will help create an economic foundation and enterprises within the Black community. Developing and carrying out our plans is of utmost importance in order to facilitate a stronger humanity and voice in society. And it is time for us as Black men to Stand Up!

INTRODUCTION

Thanks for picking up my book, **Stand Up! A Message to the Black Man.** Writing this book was very special to me because I am speaking to the heart and soul of all Black men. Because of its meaning and potential impact, it was something that I wrestled with within my spirit. My wrestling was not in the spirit of hesitancy, but rather to expose the truth and give applicable instructions for all Black men to understand in order to move into their calling. Sadly, in this society the truth does not stand as the truth, but rather if one can persuade another into believing what they want them to believe is the truth. Moreover, because of the complexities and media campaigns of society, I know that the Black man is looked upon through jaded lenses. Therefore, I conclude that the only way to change our story is to be the creators of our story. To do so, as Black men, we must peer deeply within ourselves, band together for a greater good, use our intellect to become producers of economic prosperity, and strive to climb to higher grounds in our families, communities, and societies. In our climb, some are stronger than others. That is why it is important that we continuously reach back to pull others up. And when we make it to the top, we cannot put on societal blinders and lose sight from "whence we came," because if we don't know our history, we are subject to repeat the same mistakes. With the world that we live in, there has to be a breaking point, and there MUST be a change. Hence, my subtitle, "A Message of Hope and a Call to Action!" We must plan, strategize, and plant seeds to gain control in the following areas:

- Taking control of our narrative in this society

- Respecting one another

- Creating financial independence through investment in assets and business

- Fighting against racism and injustice

- Working deliberately to change policies

- Positioning ourselves to become more involved in the political process

- Making our health a priority

- Taking the lead and responsibility for our relationships

I also wrote this book to share my story because it highlights my journey and how I experienced challenges, defeats, and victories while coming into my own. Those experiences gave me a greater awareness and appreciation of the blessings God has given to me. By telling my story, I hope to break down any challenges you may face and give you a different perspective in how to handle them. As you read, I hope you will be able to use the content as a guide to navigate through society in a purpose-driven way.

This book also serves as a support tool and guide for you as a Black man, because we all have had our ups and downs in life. If a person tells you they haven't, they are not being truthful with you. As you reflect on your life, there will be times when you might not have all the answers. This is why this book is essential as you seek to discover:

- A new direction in life

- Support and answers

- How to get up while facing failure

- How to lead in your family and community

- How to live within your purpose

- How to build an economic and financial foundation

Living life is more than just getting up, going to work, and returning home. It is about knowing and understanding our society and how it functions. For that reason, I have assembled several chapters that consider closely our history, what paths we should take to live a life of independence and freedom, and what strategic moves we should make to leverage our position as men. Chapter One of this book will cover Black America's journey in the United States. This chapter considers the rationale of why we were brought to the U.S. and how it has affected us politically, socially, and economically.

Chapter Two asks the question, 'Who am I?" This chapter discusses my upbringing and present-day life. It opens the door of my life and tells how my experiences guided my thoughts and made me who I am today, and it explores one of the fundamental questions we must ask ourselves, "Who am I?" While it might sound simplistic, the question requires you to do a great deal of reflection. It should cause you to look at your truth in terms of your moral character, self-worth, and what drives you.

Chapter Three explores planting your seed in life. It discusses the meaning of a purpose-driven life. Knowing your purpose in life opens your mind and awareness to your own blueprint and roadmap. Some people recognize their real purpose at an early age. In contrast, others go throughout life not knowing because they let the media, relationships, and lack of confidence blind them to their purpose. That anchors them down from being and operating in their true calling. This chapter will give you solutions to overcome your obstacles and will create a path for you to travel.

Chapter Four discusses distractions in life. While we cannot control what family we were born into, the circumstances we experience as children can play a role in our outlook on life as adults. It carries over into the way we think and act, and further compounds our standard of living and way of life, and it can rob you of your true purpose. This chapter will explain the different ways your true purpose could be robbed through abuse, living a lazy lifestyle, lacking a spiritual foundation, and hanging with the wrong people.

Chapter Five is about manifesting your purpose. To manifest your purpose, I explain how to develop a PLOT – Purpose, Limitation, Opportunities, and Traps. The PLOT focuses in on your purpose, highlights your limitations, gives you the ability to see your opportunities, and discusses how to see and avoid traps in your life.

Chapter Six is about exploring the various walks of life of Black men via interviews. It highlights how they experienced different circumstances and how they mapped out their path to live and be successful. Those interviewed came from different eras and different economic conditions; some were raised in single-parent homes, some two-parent homes, some military homes, and one grew up in Africa.

Chapter Seven is about being the master of your fate and the captain of your soul. Being the master of your fate requires owning the path you seek to travel, and being the captain of your soul requires having the wherewithal to make decisions that are in alignment with your moral compass. It discusses operating within faith and focus and recognizing when you are unstable. It also discusses cleaning up what you messed up and redirecting your thinking. The chapter concludes by giving tips on learning how to make money independently and investing in yourself and your family.

Chapter Eight discusses relationships and why they matter. Relationships are critical, and in this chapter I will cover the different types and protocols for each. Anything that we do in life requires some form of a relationship to expand or grow. For example, opportunities presented to my children were from relationships I established and created years ago. The same is true for one-on-one relationships between a man and woman, or couples. To reap strong returns in relationships, there must be collaboration. In addition, relationships must be honest and straight-forward. You cannot go into any relationship with an agenda that is not truthful; instead, you must go into it thinking how you could add value to the other party.

Many in the Black community are taught to acquire a college education or vocational training, and then go work for someone else.

I only partially agree with that suggestion, because getting your education does not guarantee that you will live the life you deserve, or that you will be successful.

Chapter Nine discusses creating an economic foundation for you and your community. It underscores the need to invest in stock, real estate, other assets, and business. This is one of the more important chapters because it gives different avenues for creating different streams of income and strategies for establishing an economic foundation. Chapter Ten covers wealth-creating strategies.

If you want to maximize your hopes and dreams, you must understand the political process and how it can benefit or hinder you in accomplishing your goals. Understanding the political system and how it operates will put the pieces together in understanding society and how it functions.

Chapter Eleven discusses why it is essential to participate in the political system and become a part of it by serving within it. In order to change what is happening in our community, we must become lawmakers and advocates at the local, state, and national levels to change the political landscape. And for that reason alone, Black men must become ingrained in this system. Chapter Twelve asks the question, where do we go from here, and Chapter Thirteen concludes by giving you tips; no matter what you are faced with, you keep going in life no matter what!

Given what is happening in society with the continuation of police brutality, racism, lies told as truth, and lousy policy implementation, many Black Americans are continuing the fight against a system that has planted and harvested systemic discrimination. Many are asking, "Where do we go from here?" Whatever we do as a society, Black men need to stand up and take the lead, not because of egotism or masculinity, but because it is time for Black men to carve out an extra slice of prominence and independence in this society.

As men, we all have different abilities, needs and wants. Despite our differences, the media tends to lump all Black men into a living, breathing negative stereotype. While we cannot control what people think of us, we can control how we respond to society by creating our own story. Now is the time for Black men to have a shared vision and goals that are the cornerstone to the development of ourselves, families, and communities. I pray that this book is a seed that will be planted and that those who read it will learn about their purpose by using some of the tools discussed in this book. I know we can achieve this goal, because each of us can **Stand Up! And this is my message!**

CHAPTER 1: Black America's Journey in the United States

Being Enslaved to Grow America

Black Americans in the United States have been dragged along a path that degraded, dehumanized, murdered, and undermined their liberty as human beings. They endured hundreds of years of slavery – one of the most inhumane atrocities ever instituted in the United States and the world. The first Africans arrived in the United States in 1619 as enslaved persons. Landing in Point Comfort, Virginia, Africans were stripped of their human rights and enslaved, tortured, and raped for more than 200 years. The slavers whipped the enslaved who displeased them. The white clergy preached that slavery was the will of God. Scientists "proved" that Blacks were a lesser evolved subspecies of the human race. Slavery was purely an economic endeavor to grow America and in 1793 the invention of the cotton gin solidified the importance of slavery to the South's economy. By the mid-19th century, America's westward expansion, along with a growing anti-slavery movement in the North, provoked a national debate over slavery that helped precipitate the American Civil War (1861 - 1865). Although the Union's victory freed more than four million enslaved persons, the legacy of slavery influenced American history from the chaotic years of Reconstruction (1865 - 1877) to the reemergence of the Civil Rights movement in the 1950s (Ferris State University, 2020).

Before World War II, most Black Americans worked as low-wage farmers, factory workers, domestics or servants. By the early 1940s, war-related work boomed, but the social structure limited most Black Americans to lower-paying jobs. They were also discouraged from joining the military. And even though Black Americans experience continuous oppressive treatment, they believed serving in the armed forces was an opportunity to gain freedom, respect, and access to equal rights.

After thousands of Black Americans threatened to march on Washington D.C. to demand equal employment rights, President Franklin D. Roosevelt issued Executive Order 8802 on June 25, 1941. It opened national defense and other government jobs to all Americans regardless of race, creed, color, or national origin. Even though Black men and women served during World War II, they were still seen as second-class citizens under Jim Crow law. Marching as a form of protest became commonplace for Black Americans to bring to light inequalities and to demand a change for injustices. It became a useful tool during the civil rights movement.

The Second Reconstruction

From the end of World War II until the late 1960s, often referred to as America's "Second Reconstruction," the nation began to correct civil and human rights abuses that had lingered in American society for a century (United States House of Representative History, 2020). The Civil Rights movement was a struggle for social justice in the 1950s and 1960s for Black Americans to gain equal rights under the law in the United States. The Civil War had officially abolished slavery, but it didn't end discrimination against Black people; they continued to endure the devastating effects of racism, especially in the South. By the mid-20th century, Black Americans had more than enough of prejudice and violence against them. Along with many sympathetic white Americans, they mobilized and began an unprecedented fight for equality that spanned more than two decades. Below are notable Civil Rights legislation decisions:

- In 1954, the Civil Rights movement gained momentum when the United States Supreme Court made segregation illegal in public schools in the case of Brown v. Board of Education. In 1957, Central High School in Little Rock, Arkansas, asked for volunteers from all-black high schools to attend the formerly segregated school.

- On September 9, 1957, President Eisenhower signed the Civil Rights Act of 1957 into law, the first major civil rights legislation since Reconstruction. It allowed the federal prosecution of anyone who tried to prevent someone from voting. It also created a commission to investigate voter fraud.

- President Lyndon B. Johnson signed the Civil Rights Act of 1964—legislation initiated by President John F. Kennedy before his assassination—into law on July 2nd of that year. Reverend Dr. Martin Luther King, Jr. and other civil rights activists witnessed the signing. The law guaranteed equal employment for all, limited the use of voter literacy tests, and allowed federal authorities to ensure public facilities were integrated.

- After President Johnson signed the Voting Rights Act into law on August 6, 1965, he took the Civil Rights Act of 1964 several steps further. The new law banned all voter literacy tests and provided federal examiners in certain voting jurisdictions. It also allowed the attorney general to contest state and local poll taxes. As a result, poll taxes were later declared unconstitutional in Harper v. Virginia State Board of Elections in 1966. This civil rights movement opened doors for Black Americans to have equal rights in federally funded entities and society (Editors H., 2020).

Black Americans Working in Federal Jobs and Corporate America

The federal government played an essential role in building the Black middle class in the United States. It gave African-Americans job opportunities that weren't always available in the private sector. It started during World War II and the post-war years when the need for a workforce was in demand as large numbers of whites were in military-related or war production jobs. Federal government jobs gave African-Americans a chance to get a slice of the American dream, said Frederick Gooding Jr. (Gooding, 2018). "One of the pull factors was a good government job had stable pay, higher pay, and benefits in contrast to domestic jobs and tough industrial jobs," Gooding said. "After the war ended, the federal government started to take a look at what it should do because many of those black workers were still employed (Williams, 2019)."

Working in corporate America presented Black Americans opportunities to earn higher incomes. Those doors had been closed to Black Americans until the 1960s. Since that time, government systems, such as the Equal Employment Opportunity Commission (EEOC), have been put in place to track statistics in workforce diversity. Professional organizations, such as the National Black MBA Association (NBMBAA), started in order to give professional development and better access to Black professionals seeking to enter corporate America. I am the former president of the NBMBAA Kentucky Chapter. The NBMBAA presented an abundance of opportunities to Black professionals to develop their skills, expand their network, and seek career opportunities. While organizations such as the NBMBAA are in place to open doors for Black Professionals, working in corporate America is still not an equal opportunity. According to a study, Black men are paid 13 percent less than white men; Black women are paid 39 percent less than white men, and 21 percent less than white women. A recent article revealed that Blacks who work in corporate America feel marginalized, exhausted trying to be authentic on the job, and often overlooked for promotions. In addition, Black Americans endured subtle racism at work and remained virtually nonexistent in upper-management roles, creating an unsettling workplace. Moreover, African-American employees, from millennials to those nearing retirement, feel pressure to work harder to prove themselves. The study also showed the following:

- Blacks represent less than one percentage point (0.8 percent) of Fortune 500 CEOs. "With blacks making up 10 percent of college graduates, you would think there would be 50 black CEOs. But there are only four," Jain-Link said, referring to Lowe's, TIAA, Merck & Co., and Tapestry.

- Only 3.2 percent of executives and senior manager-level employees are African-American.

- On average, 58 percent of blacks indicated they feel racism in their jobs, with the Midwest having the highest percentage at 79 percent and the Northeast the lowest at 44 percent.

- Thirty-eight percent of black millennials say they are considering leaving their jobs to start their own company (Bunn, 2019).

Being Black and the Legal System

While the doors of opportunity for Black Americans have opened a little, they have not fully opened. Black America is fully aware this is their reality because of being taught that they have to run twice as fast to keep pace with their white counterparts. This is not because white people are so much smarter or innovative than Blacks. It is because the level of scrutiny on Black Americans is so much greater. It is a constant display of mistrust and misunderstanding of Black Americans. The mistrust and lack of understanding parallels to Blacks caught up in the justice system, as crime statistics show Black Americans receive harder penalties than white Americans for the same crime. This lack of trust, or act of racism, has to change, starting with the abolishment and/or amendment of policies.

War on Drugs, Privatization of Prisons, and Targeting of Black Men

In June 1971, President Nixon declared a "war on drugs." He dramatically increased the size and presence of federal drug-control agencies and pushed through measures such as mandatory sentencing and no-knock warrants. A top Nixon aide, John Ehrlichman, later admitted: "You understand what I'm saying? We knew we could not make it illegal to be either against the war or black, but by getting the public to associate the hippies with marijuana and blacks with heroin. And then criminalizing both heavily, we could disrupt those communities." "We could arrest their leaders, raid their homes, break up their meetings, and vilify them night after night on the evening news. Did we know we were lying about the drugs? Of course, we did (LoBianco, 2016)."

Public concern about illicit drug use heightened throughout the 1980s, mainly due to media portrayals of people addicted to the smokable form of cocaine dubbed "crack." Soon after President Ronald Reagan took office in 1981, his wife, Nancy Reagan, began a highly publicized anti-drug campaign, coining the slogan "Just Say No." The Reagan administration marked the start of a long period of skyrocketing rates of incarceration, credited mainly to his unprecedented expansion of the drug war. The number of people behind bars for nonviolent drug-law offenses increased from 50,000 in 1980 to more than 400,000 by 1997.

Although President Bill Clinton advocated for treatment instead of incarceration during his 1992 presidential campaign, after his first few months in the White House he reverted to the drug war strategies of his Republican predecessors by continuing to escalate the drug war. Notoriously, Clinton rejected a United States Sentencing Commission recommendation to eliminate the disparity between crack and powder cocaine sentences. Bill Clinton signed laws that pushed for tougher prison sentences and stripped prison inmates of much of their legal-defense rights.

The era of President George W. Bush also witnessed the rapid escalation of the militarization of domestic drug law enforcement. By the end of Bush's term, there were about 40,000 paramilitary-style SWAT raids on Americans every year – mostly for nonviolent drug-law offenses, often misdemeanors. While federal reform mostly stalled under Bush, state-level reforms finally began to slow the growth of the drug war (A Brief History of the Drug War, 2020).

The Obama administration has, slowly but surely, worked to reshape how America fights its **war on drugs** — to treat drugs more as a public health issue than a punitive criminal justice undertaking. Early in 2016, President Barack Obama **began** pardoning and otherwise shortening the prison sentences of hundreds of federal inmates. In November of 2016, Obama **said** he would like to treat marijuana "as a public-health issue, the same way we do with cigarettes or alcohol." Obama signed a bill that spent $1 billion over two years to combat the growing opioid painkiller and heroin epidemic — all through public health, not criminal justice, programs (Lopez, 2017).

The Trump administration threatened to take us backward toward a 1980s-style drug war. President Trump started building a wall to keep drugs out of the country and called for harsher sentences for drug law violations and the death penalty for people who sell drugs. He also resurrected the disproven, "Just Say No" message aimed at youth (Alliance, 2020).

The privatization of prisons also added to the problem of mass incarceration in the United States. For starters, the sole act of privatization of prisons presented individuals with the opportunity to make money and profit from incarceration. In fact, to make money, there has to be an operational component, that is, an inmate. Moreover, for the prison to be profitable, it has to have more inmates working various jobs.

As prison populations surged nationwide in the 1990s and conditions began to deteriorate, lawmakers made it harder for incarcerated people to file and win civil rights lawsuits in federal court, and largely eliminated court oversight of prisons and jails (Booker, 2016). Today, prisons face monumental challenges with overcrowding, mental illness, lack of proper healthcare for inmates, and the overall management structure of operating them.

The federal government is the single largest private prison user in the United States but has reduced its private prison population in recent years. However, in 2017 Attorney General Jeff Sessions withdrew an Obama-era directive to phase out private prison contracts because of concern for the federal correctional system's ability to meet future needs (Sessions, 2017).

Political influence has been instrumental in determining the growth of for-profit private prisons and continues today in various ways. Overall prison populations continue the current trend of modest decline. In that case, the privatization debate will likely intensify as opportunities for the prison industry dry up and correction companies seek to profit in other areas of criminal justice services and immigration detention. Below are key findings of the U.S. prison population.

Key Findings:

- Of the total U.S. prison population, one in 12 people (128,063) was incarcerated in private prisons in 2016, an increase of 47 percent since 2000.

- Twenty-six thousand two hundred forty-nine people were confined in privately run immigration detention facilities in 2017, a 442 percent increase since 2002.

- Federal prisons incarcerated the largest number of people in private prisons, 34,159 – a 120 percent increase since 2000.

- The largest private prison corporations, Core Civic and GEO Group, collectively manage over half of the private prison contracts in the United States with combined revenues of $3.5 billion as of 2015 (Gotsch, 2018).

For-profit prison companies exist to make money, and therefore the size and status of the country's criminal justice system are of utmost importance to them. This connection was summed up in Corrections Corporation of America's (now-Core Civic) 2010 Annual Report:

> *Our growth is generally dependent upon our ability to obtain new contracts to develop and manage new correctional and detention facilities. This possible growth depends on several factors we cannot control, including crime rates and sentencing patterns in various jurisdictions and privatization acceptance. The demand for our facilities and services could be adversely affected by the relaxation of enforcement efforts, leniency in conviction or parole standards and sentencing practices, or through the decriminalization of certain activities that are currently proscribed by our criminal laws (America).*

From Slavery to Prisons: How Current Policies Impacted Black Men

Slavery has impacted Black Americans economically, psychologically, and emotionally. Many authorities estimate the cost of slavery at more than $70 trillion. Slavery was the direct contributor to making the United States an economic power. Even though slavery ended in 1865, some would argue that it still exists systematically through policies used and through loopholes, such as the exception clause of the 13th Amendment. The 13th Amendment, ratified in 1865, says: "Neither slavery nor involuntary servitude, except as a punishment for the crime of which the party shall have been duly convicted, shall exist within the United States, or any place subject to their jurisdiction." Scholars, activists, and prisoners have linked that exception clause to the rise of a prison system that incarcerates Black people more than five times the rate of white people, and profits off their unpaid or underpaid labor (Little, 2018). This loophole, coupled with policies legislated in the War on Drugs, opened the floodgates for minorities, notably Black men, to receive more severe penalties for lesser crimes than other races that committed the same act. Black Americans have always received stiffer punishment for crimes they committed. Black Americans have consistently been the recipients of trumped up and rigged acts of punishment. For instance, during the Jim Crow era, Black Americans were often lynched for offenses rigged through the courts.

While modern mass incarceration began in the 1970s, the Clinton administration's three-strikes law of 1994 significantly increased the prison sentences of persons convicted of a felony or previously convicted of two or more violent crimes or serious felonies. This policy opened the life sentence door to many of those convicted of previous offenses, disproportionately affecting many Black men. This policy had enormous consequences, and in 2020, the mass incarceration of Black men and other minorities was seen as unethical, calling for reform. This policy alone has affected the African-American community socially and economically. The effects of incarceration are consequential for families and communities of those individuals:

- More than one out of every six Black men today between 25 and 54 years old has disappeared from daily life. Incarceration and early deaths are the main drivers behind their absence. A history of imprisonment has been linked to vulnerability to **disease**, a greater likelihood of **cigarette smoking**, and even **premature death**. Their absence from the community removes voters, workers, taxpayers, and more.

- Children whose parents are involved in the criminal justice system suffer from psychological strain, antisocial behavior, suspension or expulsion from school, economic hardship, and are six times more likely to be involved in criminal activity.

- Partners of incarcerated individuals suffer from depression and economic hardship (NAACP, 2020).

The effects of policies that increased mass incarceration have caused a snowball effect that further complicated the Black community and family challenges. Those most affected are males being born not knowing how to become a man. I believe, just like it could be a challenge for a man to raise a girl, it is difficult for a woman to raise a boy. The presence of a man around a growing boy is impactful to his life through socialization, in both a positive and negative way. If a man is in the house and his son sees him honorably making his way in society, his son would more likely follow that same path. The same is true for a male child in a negative environment, such as a Black man involved in illegal activity. It could devolve into a situation somewhat like the movie from the 1990s, *Menace to Society*. *Menace* chronicled the fictional character Caine growing up in a home where his father killed a man, in the home. And Caine's friends also were bad influences on him. The movie had a bad ending for both the father and Caine.

The reality is that each person is a product of his environment, and, when you are raised under negative circumstances, the cards are stacked against you reversing that trend. I am not saying this to place anybody in a box, because God has a special calling for each of us. I am saying there needs to be a change because, more often than not, we witness the negative behaviors in the Black community and it becomes a cancer. In order to get rid of this cancer, there must be an adjustment in our thinking, values, and practices. Moreover, with societal discrimination, incarceration, and self-hate, generations of Black men have been growing up not knowing who they are or where they are going. I believe in order to change your circumstances you must first understand who you are as a man, and what factors influenced your current circumstances.

CHAPTER 2: Who Am I?

Our upbringing, achievements, friendships, relationships, and failures help to shape who we are. What weighs heavily upon us is the parental guidance we receive and what we experience while growing up. The neighborhood I grew up in was in West Louisville and was relatively peaceful. As I see it, my parents provided a good living for me because I had a shelter over my head, food on the table, and clothes to wear. They took a sincere interest in me. Being involved with church and having a spiritual life was ingrained in my everyday life. My mother, the nurturer of the family, made sure we read Scripture and prayed throughout my upbringing.

As Mom would say, I was always into something and she had to watch after me because I was always inquisitive. She recalled some of the things I got into. Once I climbed into the medicine cabinet and took a lamp apart. While disassembling it, the electricity started to transmit through me, and if it were not for my sister Janet grabbing me, my life would have been cut short. To this day, I still have a mark on my finger because I took apart a lamp while it was still plugged into the wall.

I was always thinking and looking for what I saw as challenges, and ways to overcome them. As early as age 11 I wanted to make money, so I started shoveling snow in the winter and mowing lawns in the summer. At the age of 12 I wanted to learn how to swim, so I would go swimming every day to teach myself. My sister Stephanie would look at me as if I were crazy as I came home with red eyes and tanned skin. She later revealed she would never have to worry about me because of how I would go after what I wanted once I set it in my mind. My competitive attitude carried me over to playing football.

My Beginning in Football

At the age of 12, I did not know much about or fully understand the game of football. All I knew was that people tackled each other while the offense tried to score a touchdown. Seeing all the hitting and tackling excited me, so I went out for the neighborhood football team, the R.E. Jones Saints. Even though I was excited, I was shy starting out in football because hitting and tackling was a new experience for me. Because of my inexperience and shyness for the game, I did not play much. By not playing much, I faced criticism and jokes from my cousins. They would say, "You are warming the bench and how many splinters did you get out of your backside." They would laugh and joke, but the jokes did not bother me. What bothered me was when my coach said, "Benson doesn't want to play football because he is a sissy!" That infuriated me! After the season, I wanted to quit, but my spirit did not allow me. I had something to prove, to myself first, then to my teammates and coaches. That next season rolled around, and I came out with an attitude of determination to solidify who I was.

After warmups, we started with tackling drills. When it was time for me to participate in drills, I ran over the defenders, to the surprise of the coaches. They quickly took notice and congratulated me. I maintained that level of aggression throughout summer camp. When it was time to place players on 1st and 2nd string, I earned the starting center position on the offensive line. While it was not the prettiest of jobs, I was a starter, and most importantly, I conquered the notion that I was a sissy and gained the respect of my teammates and coaches.

Early on in life, I learned if there was something that I wanted, I could obtain it, but I had to work for it.

My energy and excitement for football did not always carry over into the classroom. While in the 7th grade, I received a D in my science class, and after my father reviewed my grades, he calmly said that I wasn't playing football the next year. Because of how he said it, I did not take him seriously and thought he would forget. When football season began, I needed a parent's signature to play. I approached him and he asked me, "You don't remember me saying you're not playing football?" That was the end of the discussion. Knowing he was a man of his word, I made the honor roll that entire 8th grade year. Because of that experience, I would tell my friends that my father put me on Proposition 48 (college players sitting out a year because of not meeting the minimum requirements to play) before it ever was instituted.

My football-playing days extended into high school at Valley High School. As a freshman, I played both junior varsity and varsity. From my sophomore to senior year, I started and played varsity. I also ran track. I never wanted to be on the sidelines watching any games, so I did what was necessary to gain a starting role. Looking back, I would say that I was very competitive. In addition to football and track, I was on the powerlifting team. I set school records in powerlifting, and was in the *USA Today* newspaper for winning the King of the Bluegrass Powerlifting competition in my weight class. I also was in Navy Junior ROTC, where I served as the company commander during my freshman year. One of the highlights of being the company commander that year was winning the rifle competition. I was excited because I beat the upperclassmen.

During my senior year, I started dating who would later be my wife, Doris. Like all relationships, we would go to the movies and places high schoolers would hang out. I enjoyed going to the movies and sometimes to the high school clubs. Going to the clubs was and still is not my idea of having a good time.

Dating required money, and at first I asked my parents to borrow their car and give me money. After a couple of times asking for money, my father pulled me aside and said he would not put gas in his car and give me money for me to go out and date. And when, again, Dad said something, he meant it. There was no questioning him. His telling me no let me know I had to make some money, so my friends and I got a job at *The Courier-Journal* newspaper going door-to-door selling subscriptions for the paper. Working at *The Courier-Journal* was fun and adventurous because there was never a dull moment. It also was a job where I learned how to sell. The job paid an hourly rate plus commission, and the incentives were high. I would not say I was the best salesman, but I could handle my business and get the top salesman of the month periodically. Nonetheless, for a high schooler in 1987, working part-time and not having any bills, the money was good. I would make as much as $300.00 a week. Working at *The Courier-Journal* extended over into my college days.

My College Days

I decided to attend Eastern Kentucky University (EKU). I was excited to go there because it was a new beginning for me. Being away from home would provide me a certain level of freedom. I had letters from some schools that expressed interest and wanted me to play football, but my sights were not entirely set on playing football. There was so much that schools could offer a college student. Before attending college, I had my sights set on becoming a member of Alpha Phi Alpha Fraternity, Inc. My interest in becoming an Alpha man began when I would stay with my cousin, Larry, during my high school spring break at Western Kentucky University. During that time, I would hang around him and his fraternity brothers, and they would always boast how great their fraternity was and the great prominent members, such as Martin Luther King, Jr., Andrew Young, Jesse Owens, Thurgood Marshall, Maynard Jackson, and the list goes on and on. That really caught my attention. My way of thinking at that time made me question what attracted great men like them to this organization, as I saw a consistent pattern of leadership. I concluded it was something about Alpha Phi Alpha's teachings and spirit, and because of that, I wanted to be part of it.

I arrived at EKU with the mindset of learning more about myself and becoming a part of college life. My first semester was full of learning and exposure. I met new friends, such as Kevin. Kevin was an upperclassman and we immediately connected. We connected because we both were from Louisville and wanted to pledge Alpha. He showed me the ropes of a college campus, and he knew many of the Alpha members. At that time, the Alphas at EKU did not have a chapter. Many years went by with members trying to establish one, but the chapter never got off the ground for one reason or another. Looking back, I believe that everything happens on its own time, providing an answer as to why the chapter was not created earlier. The brothers that went before me established a solid foundation and practices for being Alphas. For that reason alone, I feel indebted to the members that came before me, because they laid a solid foundation and a great legacy.

Kevin and I pledged Alpha together, crossing April 10, 1988. Because we did not have a chapter at EKU during our "pledge-ship", we pledged and crossed at the University of Kentucky. On December 10, 1988, our chapter was established at EKU, and eight members, including myself, were the charter members. It was a great accomplishment because it gave us an official voice at EKU as a fraternity. Being official on campus improved our brand as an organization and increased the interest among young men wanting to become members. Having increased interest among the men on campus was critical because some did not want to pledge a fraternity that was not on campus. Some people told me they did not pledge Alpha because we did not have a chapter. I respected their decision, but as for myself, I knew that I wanted to be a member of Alpha Phi Alpha Fraternity, Inc. because the fraternity was much bigger than a chapter on a single college campus.

After crossing, I took in the full experience of being an Alpha. I built strong bonds with fraternity brothers, bonds that still exist today. Being an Alpha improved my popularity and standing on campus. Being in the fraternity also afforded me opportunities to travel to different campuses, meeting up with other fraternity brothers, doing community service projects, going to parties, and receiving respect for being an Alpha. To this day, my fraternity brothers and I reminisce, laugh, and thank God for our college days and how those experiences helped to shape who we are today. I had great and not-so-great experiences. One lesson that was not so great was the increased drinking and not being as focused in school as I could have been.

One of the keys to excelling in college, as I explained to my own children, is knowing when to study and not to study.

You cannot be effective in school if you are not disciplined in studying and letting the teachers know who you are. The prize doesn't always go to the fastest or smartest person, but to the one who is strategic about studying, seeking out and acquiring available resources, and establishing a rapport with instructors. I am not saying that you should fake your way through, but I am saying that you should be authentic and know when to ask for help. Part of the juggling act for me in college was knowing when to study and having instructors see the interest I had in the course, and if I needed help. Often, your instructors will give you the benefit of the doubt if they see you are genuinely trying to be the best you can be. I learned this later in my college career. This practice carries over into real life. When most people see that you are genuinely trying to be your best authentic self, they will give you that benefit of the doubt, whether that's giving you the opportunities or a level of mentorship. And in a spiritual sense, when you put your actions out into the universe, you will get a return on it.

College should be a new experience for anyone who attends, and I am a firm believer that one should not enter college to only go to class. I encourage everyone to participate in activities and get involved with various groups. Fraternities and sororities are not for everyone and there are many other activities to choose, such as student government groups, religious groups, or community service organizations. Being a part of groups and organizations not only gives you balance while in college, it also presents the opportunity to establish relationships that can carry on throughout life, but you have to know how to manage your time and be disciplined, or you can get off balance.

Being off-balance was very recognizable to me because of my upbringing. I was raised to carry myself with integrity and to treat others the way I wanted to be treated. I knew deep in my conscience and spirit that I was not being the best I could be, so I decided to sit out the spring semester of 1989 to get back on track. I was not planning to go home and just work or sit around, so I joined the United States Marine Corps Reserves.

My Time in the United States Marine Corps

My interest in the military began while serving in the Navy Junior ROTC at Valley High School. I always said to myself that I wanted to join the military. At that time, my thinking was that the military could further help me build my character and career, and in December 1988, I was sworn into the Marines. Before signing, my parents asked me why I wanted to join the Marines, and I told them that I wanted a challenge. Knowing all branches of service play a vital role in preserving and maintaining democracy within the U.S. and abroad, I always viewed the Marines as an elite force and the hardest of all branches. That view of being the most demanding branch of service attracted me to them.

In January 1989, I went to Paris Island, South Carolina, for basic training. I had always heard bootcamp tales, and this was before social media like YouTube, so I could only rely on the stories. I arrived at Paris Island around 2:45 a.m. Upon arrival, a drill instructor got on the bus and hollered for everyone to shut up! He shouted, "You are now in my Marine Corps!" The singing of Marine Corps songs from the recruits quickly turned to a shocking reality that life was about to change. Some of the people on the bus even started to whimper.

The drill instructor ordered everyone to hurry off the bus and place their feet on the yellow footprints outside next to the bus. After getting off the bus and lining up, we were hurried through various processing stations: getting our hair cut, getting vaccinated, turning in our civilian clothes, getting military-issued gear, etc. After being processed in, I began boot camp training, which consisted of qualifying in swimming, shooting a rifle, and passing the physical fitness test.

There is a give and take in every aspect of life. For the military, it can instill discipline, direction, and opportunities in your life. By the same token, you have to ask yourself are you willing to fight, and possibly die, for your country?

My boot camp experience was challenging for me and rewarding at the same time. It pushed me to the limits of my mental and physical state, and I passed all tests. I completed my final physical fitness test as 1st Class, scoring 294 out of 300 points, and I graduated from boot camp in April 1989 and returned to EKU in August 1989.

My Return to College

After returning to college, I felt renewed and motivated to take on the rigors of higher education. Going into the Marines enhanced my identity and improved my outlook. The new Alan was ready to get good grades and prepare for the next chapter in life. My grades and overall focus improved, and the newly formed Rho Eta Chapter of Alpha Phi Alpha Fraternity, Inc. was well on its way to lead on EKU's campus. We maintained a high grade-point average as a chapter, participated in community service projects, and won our first step show. Life was good for me because my grades had improved.

My return to Eastern surprised some because, as my fraternity brother Kevin stated, "I have seen so many of my friends come and go, meaning they would start and never return for one reason or the other." I had never intended to permanently leave Eastern because it was the place I wanted to be. At that time EKU was fun and I had made a lot of connections. There was plenty to do, with many bars and parties to explore. Looking back, I understand the social aspect of EKU presented a huge challenge for those who were not as focused or disciplined as I had become. My friends and I sometimes reflect on our time there, and as we now see it, EKU was a school that attracted a lot of first-generation students; meaning, many of the students were the first in their families to attend college. Being the first generation or sixth doesn't determine how one would succeed. However, the need for additional resources and mentoring for students, who are new to college, is necessary to assist in directing a student's focus and success in college. These resources were not readily available at Eastern. Therefore, battling the dangling carrot of endless partying interfered with many students' focus. My every intention was to remain at EKU, and graduate, until the Persian Gulf War started.

The Persian Gulf War

While on break from college, during the summer of 1990, I again worked at *The Courier-Journal* newspaper. While working there, I still attended my monthly Marine Corps Reserve duty training and two-week, active-duty training. The active-duty training was generally during the summertime. My supervisor, Thomas, was in the Army Reserves as a second lieutenant and was very accommodating to my schedule. I would never forget that day in August of 1990 when Thomas came to me and asked if I had heard that Saddam Hussein invaded Kuwait. I replied to him, "No," but I immediately felt, in my spirit, the conflict would affect me. Days later, President George H. W. Bush declared that the U.S. would hold Iraq accountable for invading Kuwait. Based on his announcement, United States troops and coalition forces began to build up forces in that region. In November 1990, I was activated for the Gulf War, arriving in Saudi Arabia in December 1990.

Being activated devastated me because of the fear of the unknown. It also devastated my family. When I first told my father, he instructed me to wait until Mom returned home to tell her. Dad was

43

not a man of much emotion, but I clearly remember seeing his face when I told him as his expression was of great concern. I told everyone else in my family, and everyone was sorrowful. My sisters cried, and I did as well, mainly because I did not know if I would live, die, or even come back home injured for life. While I was afraid of the unknown, I knew I had to go because I had signed up, which was part of my commitment and who I was as a man.

The week after Thanksgiving, Mom and Dad brought me to the formation at Fort Knox, Kentucky where I was attached to Alpha Company of 8th Tanks. I clearly remember telling them goodbye and thinking it could be the last time I would see them. Alpha Company was attached to H & S Company out of New York. The Battalion consisted of several companies that ran up and down the east coast from New York to Miami, Florida. The entire battalion's first stopping point was at Camp Lejeune, North Carolina in preparation to go to the Gulf. We arrived at Camp Lejeune a week after Thanksgiving. I experienced a hollow feeling inside as I walked into my formation, because that was now my reality.

Upon arrival at Camp Lejeune, we met up with the entire division. We went through several processing stations and procedures to prepare for our arrival and mission in Southeast Asia. When we arrived in Saudi Arabia, we continuously moved from location to location for security and strategic reasons. Our living conditions depended on where we encamped. We slept in tents, and when mobilized, we slept wherever we could, in the truck or on the ground. Physical fitness was done to maintain our stamina. Before the war started, there was a great deal of downtime. We played cards, listened to music, made calls home, and wrote letters during that time. Having downtime was needed as it took our minds off the current situation and conditions. As we moved closer to the front line, everyone's stress level increased because the risks became greater. We were on edge, even if we didn't want to admit it.

I was an enlisted soldier, and I didn't agree with all orders. Often, I spoke my mind, whether I felt an order was good or bad. In one instance, I had to do a 14-hour fire watch. Fire watch was when you had to be awake and monitor an area for safety. It was a common practice that was used in all branches of service. This particular fire watch was over a rock mine that dropped hundreds of feet into the earth. The crater stretched for about two miles, and past it was the nearest road.

In addition, we did not have any rounds (bullets) in our rifles to protect ourselves and our troops. I did my fire watch as instructed, but I adamantly expressed my frustration about the fire watch the next day. I asked and pressed the platoon leader, "How safe can we be when we don't have any rounds?" The platoon leader's reply was if an emergency happened, we should run to the Non-Commission Officer's tent to let them know. That did not make any sense to me, so I asked what type of sense that made? A terrorist could quickly approach us and immediate action would be needed. Thankfully he listened to me, and made changes in how we were equipped during fire watch. We were given rounds to protect the troops the next day.

War is hell! Being in battle will test your man or womanhood, sanity, and faith in God!

Leading up to liberating Kuwait, I recall there being at least 30 or more days of constant bombing from our aerial forces. We were on the front line and could feel the effects of the bombs. Often, we would see the bombers flying toward their targets; then shortly thereafter, we would hear the noise and feel the vibrations from the bombings. Many times, we would shout out, "Get some!" signifying the aerial forces were taking care of business. When the time came to move in to liberate Kuwait, everyone was ready to go because of the long wait. We did not know what to expect in this war because Iraq had a large Army, and the possibility of being a casualty of the war was a reality. The night before we moved in, we were allowed to make final calls home. Many did, but I decided not to because I depended on my faith to make it through the war. I held on to Hebrews 11:1, the Scripture regarding faith, where it is hoped for but not seen.

Liberating Kuwait

We all had to wear our chemical warfare equipment because of the unexpected with Hussein's regime. The common-sense belief was if he used chemical warfare against his people, he would use it against us. Moving into Kuwait occurred throughout many days and without much resistance. We took mortar fire, but the Iraqis were way off target. When we stopped in the night, it was so dark I could not even see my hand in front of my face. The darkness came from the residue of the oil well fires the Hussein regime ignited. So many oil wells were burning that it even blocked the sun from shining. I remember hearing the constant sound of bombings from airships and firing artillery. Our unit was so close to the artillery cannons, the concussions from the blast vibrated through our bodies and trucks. Earplugs did very little to soften the sound of the explosions. I am very thankful that the strategy was to bomb the Iraqis to soften their fortress and stronghold. It also opened the lanes for the ground forces to push into Kuwait. Upon arrival in Kuwait, the Iraqis had already quit because of starvation, lack of firepower, and bombing. The war was over in a matter of days.

My Persian Gulf experience forced me to again reflect on my life and who I was as a man. The thought of being home was a dream because I did not know if I would ever make it back there. I would often think about my family, friends, and the woman I dated. I thought about life and the meaning of it. I thought about why I was over there; was it for political reasons to liberate this country? I also thought about my education and where I was going academically. Through my reflection and self-awareness, I felt the need to make some changes in my life. That was when I decided to transfer from Eastern Kentucky University to the University of Louisville. It was a difficult decision because even though I felt Eastern was a home where I grew and developed many relationships, it was one chapter of my life, and at that time I needed to move to that next chapter. Sitting down and reflecting is a powerful time in your life because it presents the opportunity to do inner self-evaluation and meditation.

My "Sit-Down" Moment

Sometimes life's circumstances will force you to sit down and ask yourself, "What am I doing, who am I, and where am I going?" Your "sit-down" moments can be controllable or uncontrollable. They can consist of going to war, losing a job, getting a divorce, having an extramarital affair that results in a child, or having problems with your children. As you journey through life, you will have several sit-down moments. My first sit-down moment was going to the Persian Gulf War. I literally had to reflect on my life and its existence and its preciousness. I had to ask myself if I had treated my life as a precious gift before the war? The answer was, *not always*. The truth of the matter was I was living life as it came to me and not creating a life for myself. When I say living life as it comes, I am speaking of not being as focused as I should have been. Several situations can take control of your life: your job, relationship, or circumstance can take you off focus. By reestablishing your focus, you can establish who you are and where you want to go. Establishing who you are encompasses being faithful to God and leaning on Him to be the best man you can be to yourself and for your family.

We all fall into that trap of letting life pass us by and being out of focus. I realized that when I saw that my life could end. I assessed what I had not done, and from there, I set out to change the road I was traveling. My actions, at that time, were a common habit of sometimes neglecting how precious a gift we have until a situation disrupts it. So, do you treat your life as a precious gift? Do you guard your life against the ills of society that can wear you down? If you are not sure, look in a mirror, and ask yourself honestly, "Who Am I?"

Your Self-Discovery

When asking you to answer *Who am I?* I invite you to look inside you. Doing so could bring about self-awareness of who you are as a man and what you stand for in life. It is very tempting to try to see yourself as someone you admire. For example, while playing football in the 1980s, I admired the Nebraska football team and running back Mike

Rozier. I even wore his number while playing football throughout high school. I wanted to be like him, but I was not him. I was Alan. We all get caught up when we see people in the media or sports world, and we want to be like them. Michael Jordan was so great that they came out with commercials saying, "I want to be like Mike!" The reality is, we cannot be living as someone else because we all have our unique personalities, gifts, and talents. Depending on your position in life, it can be challenging to discover who we are and our purpose. Regardless of where you are in life and what is happening, you can always get back on the right track and live life to its fullest. It all depends on if you want to do it.

We all are born with a special purpose and it is up to us to recognize and utilize it!

Regardless of where you are in life and your age, I want you to ask God to open your mind and heart to reveal the real picture of you as a man when asking, Who Am I? It might be easy for some and difficult for others. You need to look at your authentic self and not your profession, educational credentials, or status as attachments of your character. You need to seek your core character, actions, and abilities. Some of us are born knowing who we are and where we are going. Others go through life, seeking answers, or even letting others dictate how we should live. To assist you in navigating through this process, I want you to answer the following questions.

- **What am I good at doing?** Reflect on what you are good at; for example, do you sing well? Are you good at speaking, writing, or building up others?

- **What would I fight for and what do I believe in?** Are you, for example, seeking reparations, justice for all men, for your family, etc.?

- **Do I trust myself?** Are you disciplined to do the right thing in relationships, on the job, and in life?

- **What do I value in life?** Are material possessions, education, or character what you value?

- **How do I treat myself when I fail?** Do you take failure as a learning experience and turn to others to work through that failure or do you just quit?

- **What company do I keep?** Do you hang around like-minded people or people who have your back?

- **What people have I helped in the last week?** Do you get involved in helping others?

- **What goals have I accomplished in the past two years?** Do you have goals and have you worked on achieving them?

CHAPTER 3: Planting Your Seeds of Life

Building Onto My Life's Journey

I had a blessed and secure life growing up because I had two loving parents who wanted the best for me. Mom and Dad made sure that I had all my needs and some of my wants. As I previously mentioned, the structure in our home included chores that had to be completed and devotion time, and it helped to lay the foundation of my life's journey. My parents were married more than 55 years until my mother's death in September 2016, and they kept their relationship separate from the rearing of us. Going to church and devotion time were priorities in our house as we went to Sunday School, church, and Bible study on a regular basis. Going to college was an expectation, not a dream. Education was essential in our household, and my parents paid for all of us to attend college. As my father would say to us, he would allow us to get an education; the rest was up to us.

My upbringing does not mean that I came from a fully functional family with all of our needs and wants met because we had our fair share of disappointments and challenges. Nor does it mean that being raised in a two-parent home has more stability than a single-parent household because I know plenty of brothers and sisters raised in various parental circumstances who are great and successful people in their own right. Quite frankly, as I see it, no family is fully functional.

People are raised in various families and circumstances and have different perspectives because of our socialization. Our socialization helps to shape how we communicate, interact, and respond to multiple situations. We are sometimes influenced by what we hear and see. That goes for what is happening in our homes and neighborhoods. The socialization early on begins the building process of who we are, what we are, and how we think. Growing up in West Louisville, I saw my father and mother going to work. My mom decided to work after I was born, and she worked part-time as a jeweler. My dad began his career as a custodian at Kosair Hospital in the late 1950s. He later became a brace shop technician. After working there for years, and with encouragement from my mother, Dad went to college and obtained his business degree. He was later promoted to Director of Orthotics and Prosthetics. After various mergers and acquisitions, my father retired from Norton's Hospital in 1997. When asked what he enjoyed most about his role, he said it was helping people, and he was doing just that.

Seeing Life Through the Eyes of a Black Male Teenager

Through my lens as a teenager growing up in West Louisville, I saw men working at various jobs in various positions. My father and the men in my neighborhood were married and they worked. They were engineers, educators, firemen, and laborers. In my neighborhood, everyone knew and trusted each other. For example, when we would leave for vacation, Dad would let our neighbor know we were leaving and ask him to please keep an eye on our house. Neighbors would gladly do so because everyone respected each other and their property. We respected each other's property so much that my parents taught us not to walk on our neighbors' grass.

When I became a senior in high school, my friends and I would sneak and do things our parents had forbidden. We would drink beer, hang out, and do whatever curious young men would view as exciting. Getting beer was not hard since we could get someone older than us, from the neighborhood, to buy it for us. Some of my friends would smoke marijuana, and while I would drink sometimes, I never got into smoking weed.

My friends knew I really loved sports, and because of my speed and strength, they would make jokes by calling me Clark Kent (Superman). It did not offend me because that's how we played around with each other. Everyone in the crew had a nickname, and the jokes on each other were brutal. We still laugh today about the jokes and games we played with each other. All in all, we respected each other because we knew we had each other's back.

My upbringing and the community I lived in helped to shape who I am. I saw men doing the right thing by choosing to work, to marry, and to raise their children. Seeing my father work and excel in his profession gave me a blueprint for how a man should operate to take care of his family. I knew at a young age if I wanted something, I had to work for it. I wanted to make some money, so I started shoveling snow and cutting grass at the age of 11. Doing those tasks gave me the discipline and negotiating skills, and those skills carried over to other jobs. While observing and doing various tasks that helped shape my beliefs, habits, and values, life's challenges presented new twists where I had to rely more on my faith to obtain direction and see more clearly.

Open Your Eyes to Recognize Your Blessings and Who You Are

The journey of life can sometimes be an endless maze for one striving to make it. Sometimes, you blame yourself for what's happening, which might not be the case. I am not saying that you should not hold yourself accountable. I am saying you should look at where you are, such as the environment, and determine how those forces interact and impact you. The truth of the matter is, you could be a talented individual, but your talent might not manifest because you are operating in a lion's den.

A lion's den could be in your home, the people you hang around, or what is in your mind. Be mindful in recognizing when you are in it.

How you end up in the lion's den might be circumstantial and part of your journey in life. To be mindful that you are working in the lion's den requires you to know where you are, and it tests who you are. If you fail to see and gain a better understanding of where you are, you could experience continuous setbacks throughout life. When that happens, you either internalize setbacks and build more dissatisfaction, you lose hope, and you become depressed, or even worse.

To break this cycle, you must open your eyes to see what is happening. When I say open your eyes, I am speaking of knowing who you are, where you are, what blessings you have in front of you, and what possible obstacles you must negotiate. It requires reliance on faith and spiritual guidance from the Lord to protect and show you the way. It involves the self-discovery of seeing the whole picture, the causes of it, and the consequences. Once you put all the pieces together in terms of who you are, you will become closer to understanding your purpose.

Finding Your Purpose Within

God put you here for a purpose, and we all were born for a particular purpose, with unique gifts and abilities. When exploring who you are and your purpose, you have to look at your values and what drives you in life. Having values is about having a set of standards in life, and what is driving you determines what energizes you in life. Some of us were born to change society, such as Martin Luther King, Jr. and Mahatma Gandhi. Others are born to be preachers, educators, doctors, engineers, or physicists. Even while we work within a given profession, our purpose might be to operate within that profession's confines. For example, my purpose is to educate, empower and to uplift society; and this mission covers various areas in my profession.

For instance, I am a business owner, and within that scope of work I work with clients by empowering them in leadership, management, and operating a business. I also am a college professor. I empower students to deliver and give them one-on-one coaching. The Lord has equipped me with specific tools. My educational background, work experience, and life occurrences are the tools I use to carry out my purpose. I must admit that discovering my purpose did not occur until later because I was chasing who I thought I should be instead of pursuing what God intended for me to be. Admittedly so, many of us fall into that trap of chasing the dollar instead of chasing our purpose. I am not saying to bypass an opportunity if it is a good fit for you. I am saying it should be in alignment with your purpose, with the direction you are going in life.

Why Knowing Your Purpose Matters

Asking one about their purpose could be challenging because people typically do not ask about or explore their purpose; instead, it is acted out naturally. For example, we can all see that LaMar Jackson is a special National Football League (NFL) player because of his athletic talent, and there is no need to question if excelling in football is part of his purpose. We can all see that he is great. It is not hard to see a person like LaMar Jackson's purpose, but how do you know your purpose? The tricky part of understanding our purpose is we think it should be a world-changing journey that changes millions of lives, and if that is not what happens, it is not our real purpose. We believe it should be on the level of what LaMar Jackson is doing in the NFL. That is not always the case because your mission is for a different purpose, circumstance, people and community.

Recognizing your purpose sometimes occurs immediately. At other times it occurs later in life. This discovery also could be manifested through positive or negative occurrences or a tragedy. That is the enigma of life because we sometimes learn about different aspects of ourselves at different times. That is called experience. To bring a clearer perspective on one's purpose, I surveyed a group of individuals. Of those surveyed, I asked if they were living in their life's purpose. Sixty-seven percent felt that they were, and 16 percent felt they were not living within their purpose. Eighteen percent were not sure if they were or were not living within their purpose. For those that felt they were operating within their purpose, 39 percent thought they discovered their purpose while working in their career job, and 30 percent were not sure when they discovered their purpose. Eleven percent felt they discovered their purpose at an early age or in college. Nine percent discovered their purpose as a teenager.

Eighty-six percent felt operating within their purpose is key to success. Six percent did not believe living within their purpose is key to success, and eight percent were not sure. More than 55 percent felt living within their purpose is extremely important, and 33 percent felt it was very important. More than 52 percent of the respondents felt having a purpose occurs naturally and 48 percent felt it occurs when one receives the right nurturement while growing up. Forty percent felt that one's purpose is a journey through self-discovery, and 35 percent felt one's purpose is discovered from the successes and failures in life.

Your purpose is not always meant to change the masses, but it is still grand in its context. For example, you might be a case manager who works with a man who is on drugs. Through your intervention and care, you turned his life completely around; he got stable employment, married, and raised a family. His children followed suit and raised children who are career-focused and able to make society-changing contributions. Now, if this person stayed on drugs, his life more than likely would have gone in a different direction. If he got married, there more than likely would be more discord in the relationship, thus putting stress on it. That case manager did not necessarily change millions of lives, but his impact is monumental because he changed the course of a person headed down a destructive path, or even worse, ending his life. Your calling as a case manager would be a pebble hitting the water and seeing the ripple grow larger and larger. Your counseling is impactful and it grows and grows.

We all have a particular purpose, and our journey in life either ignites a self-discovery at an early age or a later age. It can be manifested *through* our upbringing, just as it can be taken away *because of* it. The enigma of discovering your purpose can occur in a nurturing or abusive environment. However, I believe that those who grow up in a nurturing environment have a better chance of discovering their purpose because of the affirmation, learning, structure, and accountability administered. While the cards might appear to be stacked against one who grows up in unfortunate circumstances, it does not mean they will not discover their purpose.

CHAPTER 4: Distractions in Fulfilling Your Purpose

The journey through life will bring some rewards, challenges and failures that build who you are. Those rewards sometimes could give you a high and make you forgetful of the past, while the challenges and failures could have a larger blow to your entire well-being. Sometimes when you are at a low point in your life, you have no other choice but to look from within and ask, "How did I contribute to this happening?" That moment for me occurred when I went through separation and divorce. This situation was different from my first "sit-down" moment when I was in the Persian Gulf because I was not prepared for separation and divorce, mainly because of my idealistic view of marriage. It was a naive way of looking at how the dynamics of relationships operated because, frequently, we are guilty of comparing relationships, whether it be through our friends' relationships or what we see on television. One thing that I learned and ardently believe is every relationship is different.

I was married for over 14 years, and from that union came a set of beautiful twins – Hilton and Hayley. Like any relationship, we had our good and difficult days, and both of us contributed to the growth and indifference of it. After not seeing eye-to-eye, we separated. It was an adjustment for the kids and me. The kids were with me several days a week. Seeing Hilton and Hayley was a must because they are an extension of me, and I was determined to play an active role in their lives. That was very important to me and I was willing to sacrifice for it. During that time, I had a job opportunity in California, and it was substantial in terms of pay. One of my buddies said to me, "Man, that company pays well," but I had already decided, in my head, not to accept it because I was not going to be that far away from my kids. I already knew I was not going to be a man who just sends a check for child support. I was going to be a man that was going to be present for his children.

Whether you created a child through marriage or otherwise, it is your responsibility as a man to nurture and support that child!

When we came to the point of divorce, it was not easy for me. I was embarrassed and angry, and it was something that I did not share with many people. I dated, thinking that would get me back to where I thought I should be, but I was not myself. My mom, at times, would ask me how I was doing, and I would give her updates. After telling her, she would always say to me to make sure I get Alan back in a good place. I knew she was only telling me that out of love and from a place of wisdom. She was right, and after reflecting, I would advise anyone who is going through a breakup or divorce to take the time to do self-reflection. Self-reflection is thoroughly looking at what happened in the relationship and examining the contributing factors.

I took a hard look in the mirror throughout the separation and divorce and asked, "Who am I?" I wondered whether I was made of what my values were, and what I stood for as a man. As a man, I was mentally broken and was like a ship sailing without a sail. It was always easy to blame others for why my years of marriage did not work, but I had to face the truth about myself in order to be authentic to myself. This involved: 1) Analyzing how I contributed to the success or failure of the relationship 2) Learning to accept my contribution to the decline of our relationship. I saw how the other party contributed to the relationship and how it made me feel as a man. Through my reflection, I recognized that I was not myself, nor living within my true, authentic purpose. Moving forward, there were some rules that I decided I was going to live by:

- Always selflessly make room for my life.

- Strive to be healthy and live a life of peace.

- Stick to my values, be spiritual, financially prudent, truthful, and purpose-driven.

- Always keep my eyes open, and when a person shows me who they are, believe them.

- Always treat people the way I want to be treated.

When I came to that awareness it was a new day for me. I became a new and improved man because refining who I was uplifted my spirit and redefined me. It placed me back on track toward fulfilling my purpose.

Going through my experience helped me to take a hard look at myself, and I know that I am blessed that I came out of it with a better understanding of myself, and a better attitude. That is not always the case because of what we experience and how it affects us mentally and emotionally. Sadly, it could be the difference-maker for growth or destruction.

Potential Robbers of Your Purpose

I've argued there are more unsuccessful people than successful people in this society. Some of it has to do with our mental compacity. Our life circumstances, our self-esteem, and the blows we have been dealt in life. Through our circumstances, many of us do not know, learn, or live out our purpose because how we were socialized carries over into our adult life. Sometimes it's because what we've experienced while growing up remains with us throughout life. What you experience can affect the person you are and rob you of your purpose.

We cannot change who our parents are, what occurs inside our home, and how we were raised. Being in an abusive home can be a roadblock in recognizing our real purpose. It can be devastating to our mentality, outlook on life, and self-worth. Abuse is just one of the various ways of robbing you from discovering and carrying out your true purpose in life. Other ways that could affect you is lacking exposure, living a lazy life, having an indifferent mentality, lacking a spiritual foundation, hanging with the wrong people and choosing the wrong mate.

Abuse

Abuse comes in many forms. It's physical, mental, emotional, and sexual, just to name a few. It could come from parents, siblings or friends. We all respond differently to abuse and different challenges in life because of our psychological makeup. I have personally witnessed abuse within my family and with friends and the abuse was inflicted by both men and women. One could take abuse as fuel to motivate them to demand change in their circumstances. The opposite also happens. Those who seek change strive for it because they imagine life better than how they currently live. In either case, the abuse can be internalized in that person, which affects how they treat others. This form of behavior can carry over in relationships, marriage and the rearing of children.

As you can see, abusive behavior can become a huge snowball that can produce significant damage and consequences. That is why it is essential to take ownership of abuse by recognizing it and getting help. It is like Alcoholics Anonymous when the first step requires you to acknowledge and admit that you are an alcoholic.

Lack of Exposure

Being open to exposure is the ability to see the world, different opportunities, and people who are different from you. Some would equate exposure to the amount of money one possesses, but you can gain exposure in many ways regardless of your income level. One way of gaining exposure is through the internet as well as in your studies. By increasing your exposure, you will see the beautiful things life offers and the various qualities different cultures bring. Exposure gives you a different perspective in terms of how the world operates and who you are. Learning who you are does not mean that you are better than the next person; it refines your meaning and heritage. It only means that we all are different in unique ways.

Living a Lazy Lifestyle

The practice of laziness can become habit-forming. <u>Proverbs 19:15</u>, states: "Laziness casts one into a deep sleep, and an idle person will suffer hunger." This parallels what my mother said to me, "When I was growing up, you either worked or you starved." This habit-forming activity can rob you of gifts and opportunities that are in front of you. Laziness can be carried over from family to family since it breeds a spirit of complacency and dependency. I am not saying this to belittle anybody, and I believe we all have moments of "slumber" in our lives. In either case, you have to know when to take care of business and when to relax. It is a dogma that I have instilled in my children.

The best way to break away from this habit is to get up and move with direction and to develop a schedule by writing your daily activities. You need to establish goals, and once you have completed each activity, check it off as completed. It is a system that will lock you into a pattern both physically and mentally of doing and staying on task. For your mind to be triggered to do this task unconsciously, it takes months of practice.

Having an Indifferent Mentality

Some years ago, Allstate Insurance Company introduced a character called Mayhem. Mayhem is quite funny and very destructive because as long as Mayhem hung around, what could go wrong did go wrong. Our mentality can be just as destructive. We all have a mentality. How we were raised, what we value, and how we see ourselves establishes our mentality. Some of us have a limited mentality, while others have an open mentality. Persons with a closed mentality see things only through the lens of their own reality. They do not see beyond what they can physically see. They could be fixated on an altered reality.

Your mentality and outlook on life can open doors of opportunity for you or burn many bridges.

This type of mentality will rob you of securing various opportunities that the world has to offer. It also builds up layers of mental and physical roadblocks. Conversely, one with an open mentality sees reality and also sees alternatives and possible solutions to a situation. Having an open or closed mentality has nothing to do with race, class, income status, or political party, but more so with respect for all humanity.

Lacking a Spiritual Foundation

Your spiritual foundation is what anchors you in life. Having a solid foundation will help secure you when those storms come into your life. It gives you the ability to stand up and walk through storms with faith, guidance, and courage. Having storms is a natural occurrence. As I tell my friends, as we get older we all should have a story to tell about how we fought through various storms and came out victorious. Having a weak spiritual foundation is like a plant planted in the sand. When the storm comes, we cannot weather the storm because we do not have anything to stand on. When the winds blow, we will go in any direction the wind is blowing, just like the plant. You can see the two differences between having a solid or weak foundation.

Hanging with the Wrong People

When I was growing up, my parents wanted to know who my friends were and who their parents were. I could not just get up and leave the house and stay out all night because I had to be in the house by the time the streetlights came on. As a child, I did not understand that, but now I know. My parents weren't trying to place me on a pedestal or to shelter me; they just wanted to protect me and teach me about with whom to associate. If a child was a troublemaker, my parents prohibited me from hanging out with him because they did not want me to be around any negative influences. Moreover, hanging with the wrong crowd could become habit-forming and your new standard could eliminate the conscience of doing the right thing.

Having the Wrong Mate/Partner in Your Life

Years ago, Tina Turner came out with the song, "What's Love Got to Do With It." The song was soulful with a lot of meaning because we all have experienced the joys and, sometimes, the failures of relationships. I believe for any relationship to be successful, there must be work-involved collaboration. Sometimes the work and cooperation might be titled, in that one person might be doing 70 percent of the work and the other 30 percent. Regardless of who is carrying the greater or lesser load, what is important is that both understand their role in that relationship's grand scheme. What breaks down relationships is when one has a plan that impacts it negatively. Moreover, the lack of clear communication is something that would render negative consequences in a relationship. Having an alternative agenda in a relationship also could rob your mate's ability to grow into his full potential. Through my divorce, I have done a great deal of self-reflection, received counsel and discussed the dynamics of relationships with various people. I advise having your eyes wide open at the beginning and throughout the relationship. It's not about trying to determine your mate's negatives. It is about learning more about your mate. Your mate will show you who they are. And when someone shows you who they are, please believe them.

Who you choose as your mate can either be the wind beneath your wings or an anchor that will keep you at a standstill or drag you down further.

To break this cycle of abusiveness, laziness, and nonsupport of a significant other, you must be able to recognize what is happening and take ownership of it. To take ownership, look in the mirror and ask yourself how you contributed to this situation. Even if any problem is 80 percent their fault or 20 percent yours, you contributed to it to a certain degree, and sometimes you might discern you were the main contributor. At other times, you might need a third party to counsel you to bring about more awareness of the actions taking place in your relationship. At some point you should ask yourself how you can correct it and what you learned from it.

CHAPTER 5: Manifesting Your Purpose

We all are born with specific abilities, gifts, and talents. Some of us discover our gifts and aim to cultivate and use them at an early age while others discover their gifts later in life. Sometimes we operate within our gifts but get off course because of a life circumstance. As discussed in the previous chapter, there are a plethora of reasons why that could be. Whether you discovered your gift at an early age or are just realizing it, it requires work for it to blossom. A good example is Michael Jordan, the great NBA basketball player. Some would argue that he is the best player ever to play in the NBA, but how did he become great? He became great because of his failures, and from his failures he worked extremely hard at getting to where he wanted to be. If you were on MJ's team, the expectation was for you to work just as hard as he did to be your best as well. And for that reason, his teammates elevated their performance and that is why they won championships. The same is true for Tiger Woods. To become great, he would hit over 1,000 balls every day. Even at a low point in his life his determination and work ethic did not let him quit, and he rebounded to the level of greatness. And it looks like his son, Charlie, is on the path to becoming great in the game of golf as well.

To have our gifts, skills, and talents blossom, we must work and continuously practice. As we witnessed Michael Jordan and Tiger Woods amaze crowds with how they raised their performance levels. They worked extremely hard to accomplish those milestones by capitalizing on their God-given talent. To center in and elevate our gifts, we must discover and evaluate our true gifts and take steps to enhance them.

My PLOT: Purpose, Limitations, Opportunities, and Traps

Many have heard people or read books about people operating within their purpose. By operating within their purpose, they are operating within their gifts. On Sundays, while having dinner at my parents' house, my sister Stephanie would ask us if we knew our purpose. By her asking, the looks on our faces showed we had to think about the question. The truth of the matter is I am a firm believer that if you ask ten people their purpose, seven out of 10 would find it challenging to answer without thinking it over and struggling to come up with an answer. And in all fairness to Stephanie, I believe she was not asking to try to put us on the spot, but rather to plant a seed of thought into our minds.

Much of it again depends on our self-discovery and our socialization in life. Our self-discovery is that what we like is what we want to be. For example, I have asked many students what they want to be in life. Many of them would say they wanted to play in the NFL or NBA. I would then ask them, what if they did not make the NFL or NBA; did they have any alternative plans? What would they plan to do? Many of them did not have an answer. I then explained to them my reason for asking was not to cast doubt on their dreams but rather to bring to light the need to have a backup plan. I also explained they needed to discover their natural gifts and passion, get a quality education, and perfect their abilities. I would tell them that it is a must to surround themselves with people who give them guidance and support. I emphasized the importance of seeking wise counsel. For them to truly get on track with who they were, they needed to PLOT out their lives. To assist them in determining their gifts, I created a system called a PLOT.

A PLOT is a self-reflection map that lists your Purpose, Limitations, Opportunities, and Traps. It aims to focus on your purpose by looking at factors that could affect your life. Implementing your

PLOT requires you to evaluate your life's experiences to determine why and where you are today. For example, I once heard a Toyota executive speak about his upbringing and life experiences. He gave an excellent presentation as he discussed how his experiences, the challenges he overcame, and how people in his life helped shape who he is today. He further explained while he was afforded access to various opportunities, it was the challenges that tested his courage and determination to achieve. Those challenges also made him a wiser person. Like the presenter, we all have had numerous experiences, people in our lives, and challenges that influenced our thoughts and direction. Those experiences, whether positive or negative, have impacted our direction in fulfilling our purpose. Regardless of where we are today, I am a believer that we must fulfill our God-given purpose.

By conducting an inventory of the jobs we've had, skills we've learned, and our other life encounters, we expediate carrying out our purpose. By completing a PLOT, it could give you clarity on who you are, your limitations, your opportunities and the roads you should not travel.

Self-Reflection

For your self-reflection to be most effective, you must be truthful with yourself, regardless of how good or bad it may appear. Below are preliminary questions you should ask yourself for a clear perspective on who you are, what you stand for, and where you are going. After answering the questions, identify what drives your decisions. Is it money, the need for acceptance, opportunity, etc.? If you are uncomfortable and unclear with any of your answers, please seek wise counsel to assist you.

- Who am I? What do I believe in? What will I not tolerate?
- What impact do I have on others?
- Have I planned my life according to my purpose?
- Have I been focused on reaching my goals?

- How do I respond when I have setbacks? Do I take setbacks as an opportunity to regroup and learn, or do I quit?

Creating Your PLOT

Your PLOT is designed to explore and bring out your passions, limitations, opportunities, and traps on your journey. Like the above questions, this process will require you to reflect on and conduct an inventory of yourself. Below are examples of questions you should ask yourself:

Purpose

- What task(s) do you love to do?

- What are your natural talents and skills?

- What is extremely easy for you to accomplish, that others find difficult?

- What is your brand, and what do others say are your talents?

- What sets you apart from others?

Limitations

- What task(s) have you repeatedly tried that are challenging for you to accomplish?

- What skills do you lack that hinder achieving your goals?

- What fears do you have that preclude you from accomplishing your goals?

Opportunities

- What benefits would you receive from your career choice?

- What new technology can help you?

- What is the forecasted growth of the career/industry you are aspiring to enter?

- Who could mentor you, and what organizations could you join?

- What organizations are you a member of that could help you develop your skills and achieve your goals?

- Do you have a mentor?

Traps

- What are the challenges that could hinder you from accomplishing your goal(s)?

- Is your career/job/industry stable, transforming, or becoming obsolete?

- Is the economy affecting you and keeping you from achieving your goal(s)?

- Are your fears your trap?

- Are you living in a place that hinders your growth?

By applying a PLOT to your life, it will give you more direction and focus. After gaining insight into your PLOT, develop an action plan to correct or carry out what you discovered.

Your Action Plan

After discovering your purpose, you need to develop a strategy of how to put your purpose into action. Mapping this out and following through is extremely important, since having a plan without any action is useless to achieving any goals. It also forces you to think about how you will achieve it and gives you a roadmap for doing so. To assist in guiding you through this process below is a Life Plan Matrix for your completion. Six areas itemize a series of categories and questions:

- Defining your purpose

- Obtaining educational training

- Furthering your career and/or starting a business

- Developing your brand and establishing relationships

- Managing your finances and creating wealth through assets, investments, and business

- Having a health plan

There are action steps in each category you should list. It also asks how you will achieve it. Under the *Defining Your Purpose* action item, it asks what is your purpose. Write out what your purpose is. Next, write how you will better position yourself within your purpose. For example, if your purpose is to educate and mentor young Black men to be the best they can be, achieve it by mentoring them at the local YMCA or creating a nonprofit that focuses on mentorship. Reflect on and complete each block, to the best of your ability. After completing your matrix, there will be an evaluation period where you evaluate your progress over four years. The purpose of this is for you to assess your progress. If you determine you did not make the level of improvement you sought, that would be the time for you to ask why and what needs to be completed to render a different result.

YOUR LIFE'S PLAN MATRIX PURPOSE STATEMENT		
DEFINING YOUR PURPOSE	Your statement of your plan	Your statement of how you are going to achieve your goal
What is your purpose in life?		
How are you going to maximize your purpose in life?		

LIFE PLAN MATRIX
PURPOSE STATEMENT

OBTAINING HIGHER EDUCATION	Your statement of your plan	Your statement of how you are going to achieve your goal
What are your educational goals?		
CAREER OR ENTREPRENEURSHIP	Statement of your plan	How are you going to accomplish your career goals
What career are you seeking to pursue?		

BRANDING YOURSELF AND DEVELOPING RELATIONSHIPS	Your statement about your plan	What are you going to do to brand yourself and develop relationships that will act as a bridge to accomplishing your goals?
What is your brand, and do you feel you need to rebrand yourself?		
Do you network to develop relationships, and are you comfortable in developing relationships?		
YOUR PERSONAL FINANCE AND WEALTH	Your statement about your plan	What are you going to do to achieve your financial goals?
What are your financial goals? (One's financial goals are the amount one desires to make annually, the amount of money saved, and the amount invested.)		

YOUR PERSONAL HEALTH PLAN	Your statement about your plan	What are you going to do to achieve your personal health goals?
What is your health plan? (Personal health refers to the wellness of the individual. It not only refers to the physical well-being of an individual, but it also comprises the wellness of emotional, intellectual, social, economic, spiritual, and other areas of life.)		

LIFE PLAN MATRIX
STRATEGY PLAN

PURPOSE STATEMENT	What are your strategy and execution plans?	Year 1 Goals	Year 2 Goals	Year 3 Goals	Year 4 Goals
Fulfilling Your Purpose					
How are you going to maximize your purpose in life?					
EDUCATION	What are your strategy and execution plans?	Year 1 Goals	Year 2 Goals	Year 3 Goals	Year 4 Goals
What are your educational goals?					

CAREER OR ENTREPRENEURSHIP	What are your strategy and execution plans?	Year 1 Goals	Year 2 Goals	Year 3 Goals	Year 4 Goals
What career are you seeking to pursue?					

BRANDING YOURSELF AND DEVELOPING RELATIONSHIPS	What are your strategy and execution plans?	Year 1 Goals	Year 2 Goals	Year 3 Goals	Year 4 Goals
What is your brand? Do you feel you need to rebrand yourself?					
Do you network to develop relationships, and are you comfortable in developing relationships?					

LIFE PLAN MATRIX STRATEGY PLAN					
YOUR PERSONAL FINANCE AND WEALTH	**What are your strategy and execution plans?**	**Year 1 Goals**	**Year 2 Goals**	**Year 3 Goals**	**Year 4 Goals**
What are your financial goals? (One's financial goals are the amount one desires to make annually, the amount of money saved, and the amount invested.)					

PERSONAL HEALTH PLAN	What are your strategy and execution plans?	Year 1 Goals	Year 2 Goals	Year 3 Goals	Year 4 Goals
What is your health plan? (Personal health refers to the wellness of the individual. It not only refers to the physical well-being of an individual, but it also comprises the wellness of emotional, intellectual, social, economic, spiritual, and other areas of life.)					

LIFE PLAN MATRIX
EVALUATION ANALYSIS

YOUR PURPOSE	Did you accomplish your year 1 goals? (Yes or No) Explain if you did or did not.	Did you accomplish your year 2 goals? (Yes or No) Explain if you did or did not.	Did you accomplish your year 3 goals? (Yes or No) Explain if you did or did not.	Did you accomplish your year 4 goals? (Yes or No) Explain if you did or did not.
Fulfilling Your Purpose				
How are you going to maximize your purpose in life?				
EDUCATION	Did you accomplish your year 1 goals? Explain if you did or did not.	Did you accomplish your year 2 goals? Explain if you did or did not.	Did you accomplish your year 3 goals? Explain if you did or did not.	Did you accomplish your year 4 goals? Explain if you did or did not.
What are your educational goals?				

LIFE PLAN MATRIX
EVALUATION ANALYSIS

CAREER OR ENTREPRENEURSHIP	Did you accomplish your year 1 goals? (Yes or No) Explain if you did or did not.	Did you accomplish your year 2 goals? (Yes or No) Explain if you did or did not.	Did you accomplish your year 3 goals? (Yes or No) Explain if you did or did not.	Did you accomplish your year 4 goals? (Yes or No) Explain if you did or did not.
Career Goal(s)				

BRANDING YOURSELF AND DEVELOPING RELATIONSHIPS	Did you accomplish your year 1 goals? (Yes or No) Explain if you did or did not.	Did you accomplish your year 2 goals? (Yes or No) Explain if you did or did not.	Did you accomplish your year 3 goals? (Yes or No) Explain if you did or did not.	Did you accomplish your year 4 goals? (Yes or No) Explain if you did or did not.
What is your brand, and do you feel you need to rebrand yourself?				
Do you network to develop relationships, and are you comfortable in developing relationships?				

82

LIFE PLAN MATRIX
EVALUATION ANALYSIS

YOUR PERSONAL FINANCE AND WEALTH	Did you accomplish your year 1 goals? (Yes or No) Explain if you did or did not.	Did you accomplish your year 2 goals? (Yes or No) Explain if you did or did not.	Did you accomplish your year 3 goals? (Yes or No) Explain if you did or did not.	Did you accomplish your year 4 goals? (Yes or No) Explain if you did or did not.
What are your financial goals? (One's financial goals would be the amount one desires to make annually, the amount of money saved, and the amount invested.)				

PERSONAL HEALTH PLAN	Did you accomplish your year 1 goals? (Yes or No) Explain if you did or did not.	Did you accomplish your year 2 goals? (Yes or No) Explain if you did or did not.	Did you accomplish your year 3 goals? (Yes or No) Explain if you did or did not.	Did you accomplish your year 4 goals? (Yes or No) Explain if you did or did not.
What is your health plan? (Personal health refers to the wellness of the individual. It not only refers to the physical well-being of an individual, but it also comprises the wellness of emotional, intellectual, social, economic, spiritual, and other areas of life.)				

CHAPTER 6: Building Yourself Up When All Odds Are Against You

As a Black man in America, we are often attacked and portrayed in several negative lights. We are considered thieves, hoodlums, and sex-crazed men who father babies with no care of providing any type of parental guidance or financial support. Even having amassed several educational degrees and having a blessed life, I am very aware of relational concern and fear of the police. I know all it takes for things to go the wrong way is for me to be at the wrong place at the wrong time or to move the wrong way. Those actions could render harm or death. Why do I feel that way? Because that is my reality after seeing countless incidences where black and brown people were killed by the police. The sad reality is the abuse and killings are nothing new. We now just see them in plain sight because of smartphone devices. I have never been to jail and was raised to respect authority, whether it was for an older member in my family or neighborhood or for the police. Growing up, I considered becoming a police officer and majored in Police Administration at EKU. I even contemplated going into the Secret Service. I have friends and family that serve in law enforcement, and when asked why police misconduct occurs, they would say that white officers are afraid of Black people or because of deep-seated biases. In reality, we all have fears and biases, but the problem with policing is they have the power to act out in ways which could devastate a life, and are often given the benefit of the doubt in the eyes of justice. The remedy to all of these problems varies from more accountability in policing to stricter laws. I believe in law enforcement and see it as necessary in our country and neighborhoods. People misunderstand that defunding police equates to taking away their power. I do not believe in taking away their ability to serve and protect, but I believe in holding the police accountable, and accountability starts in hiring, then training through the academy, and on the job.

When I mention accountability, I have to look at it from all angles. Whether it be local or national, I have witnessed Black-on-Black crime and its negative effects on the Black community. It is a massive problem regardless of the valiant efforts of Black people and Black organizations working to combat it. I understand this is a subject that we do not like to discuss, and the sad reality is that just by me discussing it, some of my Black brothers and sisters might accuse me of having a hidden agenda. This problem is not a Republican or Democrat problem. It is a humanity problem within our community. Until we put more effort into tackling this problem head-on, it will sadly continue to grow. There is a plethora of reasons why there is Black-on-Black crime, and there are historical and contributing factors that add to those reasons. Even though we are aware of those factors, we, as Black people, must take the lead.

Before you can hold others accountable,
you first must hold yourself accountable.

I raise both the issues of run-ins with law enforcement and Black-on-Black killing because both erode our independence, stability, and sustainability as Black men. Yes, it is true that there are way too many black men and other minorities in prison, serving harsher sentences than what their white counterparts are serving, but we don't have to kill each other. We also have to develop more love and self-respect for ourselves and one another. We have to start setting the example to have more people to admire.

Seeing the World I Live In

Growing up in the 1970s, I saw things happening that I did not understand. As a teenager in the 1980s my world consisted of going to school, church, and playing sports. I was bused at a young age in the mid-1970s, and I remember seeing the bomb fires and throngs of people protesting with stop busing signs and security guards being on the bus. I was not aware of what was happening because I did not fully understand what was going on, and being on a bus with my friends insulated any of my fears. While attending Valley High School in Louisville, Kentucky, people would shout racial slurs while I was waiting for the city transit bus. It did not bother me because I viewed them as cowards. After all, they would yell slurs while speeding by in a car. I knew there were racial and social challenges in the United States at that time; it just was not in my purview.

While in college and the United States Marine Corps, society's racial and social differences began to radiate more in my life. As time progressed in each decade, I witnessed the Black man's erosion as the head of the household, which I attribute to higher incarceration and more Black-on-Black crime which led to more single-parent homes.

Through my own personal and professional experiences and travels throughout the world, I sadly realize that race still matters here in America. You will hear some people say that we should have a colorblind society and that everybody is equal. I am not one to argue, but for those that say we live in a color-blind society, I believe they are blind to the truth. Even the United States Declaration of Independence, declares that all men are created equal, but it did not mean all people. Even framers debated the classification of Black enslaved people. The framers also decided the enslaved were not human beings but property; therefore, they put in place the 3/5 clause. The 3/5 clause stated that the enslaved were classified as 3/5 human and as property. It was not until the late 1960s that Black Americans wrestled free from Jim Crow law bondage, but still were being classified as 2nd class citizens. We are now in 2021, and I have to ask are we free or under another form of systematic bondage?

Growing up, I began to see the expanding dearth of Black men heading their homes, and I realized that more Black children were being born into single-parent households. With the crack pandemic in place, more Black men were going to prison as former President Bill Clinton instituted the three strikes Crime Bill in 1994. The bill stated if a person had two previous felonies, even if it were a nonviolent drug charge, a third conviction would result in a life sentence in prison. Bill Clinton later acknowledged he regretted signing the bill as it did more harm than good. In my summation, this bill opened the floodgates wide open for more single parents, more women being the head of households, and the Black man being out of the home. This action had and still is having a tumultuous effect on the Black household.

The Crime Bill Effects on the Black Household

My mother always stressed to me to be truthful, to walk in truth. While I know there are contributing factors that led to the black household's erosion, the Crime Bill landed a significant blow on the Black community. Its rippling effect has been devastating. We have more families headed by women and more women are grandmothers taking care of grandchildren. This is not to excuse men for not taking care of their children, but we have to ask, besides impregnating women, how can you teach a man how to father when they possibly didn't have a father around. When you have missing elements in your upbringing, it is harder to follow through on basic responsibilities. Having a man in the house and teaching a young man right from wrong makes a difference. Growing up, my father put the fear of God in my life when he talked to me about the possibility of getting my girlfriend pregnant. I was frightened, but probably more fearful of him, should something like that happen. It is essential that we, as men, go back to being the heads of our household and be the example in the home.

Young boys must have a positive male role model in their life to teach them right from wrong, and how to navigate through life.

When speaking of the absence of the Black man in our families, I am speaking of the man who naturally takes his hands and gives nurturing guidance to a growing young man, and woman. A man being in the home has positive effects on both. The boy will see a role model, and the girl will have a barometer of authentic and benevolent manhood. While I believe in the family being together, even if you are divorced or birth a child out of wedlock, it is still your responsibility to nurture your children. The guidance that our young men and women need is the type of guidance where they can learn how to make money independently, think independently, build business relationships, and protect their family.

How much of an effect does a man have on the upbringing of his son? I administered a blind survey of African-American men who were raised in a predominately two-parent home. Most of the respondents obtained either a bachelor's degree or both a bachelor and master's degree. When asked the question while growing up who were their African-American male role models, 58 percent of the respondents said their father, and 50 percent said a family member, brother, or uncle. It is part of the reality of Black men and their families. The sad fact is in America the media does not tell the whole truth, but in fact highlights the negative. As Black men, we must stop allowing the media and others to tell our story. The truth is many African-American men have attended college, graduated, and are responsible for their children; however, the focus that we primarily see from the media is the negative aspects of Black men. It is obviously by design. It is a bad design because many people believe what they see. Years ago, I remember having a conversation with a young African-American male about society and he told me a lot of the images he saw of black men were his reality because that is what he grew up around.

As a youth, there were several men I looked up to. They were relatives and attended my church. But first and foremost, I looked up to my father because he was an example of a strong man that took care of his family and was always respected by my mother. Dad also was financially savvy because he counted every penny he earned, and was very organized. He was rather quiet but his actions spoke volumes, and what he taught me helped prepare me for life and fatherhood.

The Impact of a Father

I am a father of two, a beautiful boy and girl who just completed high school and now are in college. How I raised them included some of how my father raised me. My father was a disciplinarian in my house. What he said, he meant, and I did not question him. He also was a provider. As I have stated, I had all my needs met and some of my wants. Dad and Mom provided all of us with the opportunity to go to college. While in college, my parents did not want us to work; they just wanted us to focus on our studies, get good grades, and do the right thing. In my second semester of college, as earlier noted, I pledged Alpha Phi Alpha Fraternity, Inc. After crossing over, I did not keep my grades up to my father's expectations, so when he picked me up from college and received my grades, he asked me, "Well, Alan, how will you go back to school?" He was disappointed in my grades.

I told him that I would pay for it myself, so that entire summer I worked and saved up enough money to put a down payment on my classes. Looking back, my father was trying to teach me a lesson. He taught me to follow through on what he told me. He would always say he didn't mind helping people that wanted to help themselves. The second lesson was that he wanted to see what I was going to do. He saw what I was made of because he did finish paying for my college that semester.

When I became a father how I raised my children included some of the ways and practices my father raised me. I said the word, *some*, because, while my father was, and still is an awesome dad and provider, times have changed, and as I see it, I am building onto what he taught me. Does that mean I should live a perfect life and hide all my shortcomings? No. I learned early on as a parent that it can be more positive if I showed my children I was only human and have made mistakes. By explaining some of the mistakes I made on a child's level, I felt that my children would better understand why I told them yes and no, and not to do this or that. Secondly, as a parent, holding myself accountable is vital. As a manager, my district manager said to me, "How are you going to hold others accountable and not hold yourself accountable?" That is true as a parent, friend, and in your everyday walk in life.

As a father, holding yourself accountable is crucial because children, while growing up, are very impressionable. What they see is what they like and want to be at times. For example, a lot of children dream of playing in the NBA or NFL. Why is that? It is because that is an example of success many African-Americans see. Sadly, in some communities, seeing dope dealers is something that is successful in the minds of children as well because they see them with all the material items and all the women. They see them with silk shirts, bling, fancy cars, and a lot of money to "make it rain." In the minds of young men who do not have a positive father figure who is a role model, this life could be very appealing. But why choose a route of selling drugs? In some households, children grow up not having anything to eat, no clothes to wear, homeless, or even abused by parents or someone else in the household. When you grow up in those types of conditions you are looking for a way out and just about anything that is an improvement to your current situation is a step up. This type of thinking is a reality for many. I had the nourishment, love, guidance and discipline from parents who wanted a better life for me. And the thought of me selling drugs was a death sentence, not literally, but a harsh punishment from my parents. I respected and feared my parents so much that I did not want to disappoint them. I also knew if I got into something that I had no business getting into, there would be a harsh punishment after my father put a belt on my back. In today's way of living, some of our experts would say that it was child abuse, getting a whooping from my parents, but that was a time when parents physically disciplined their children. I am thankful they punished me, because if they had not I would probably be paying some grave consequences today. Children need guidance because of their thinking capacity. Their minds are not developed enough to decipher right from wrong and what's best for them. The sad reality is that some adults have been misguided in such a way in their early life it is difficult for them to decipher right from wrong. They also don't have the confidence in themselves to make a change. It all starts with your upbringing.

Who Do We as Black Men Look Up to?

Your upbringing plays a vital role in how you turn out as an adult. It is not to say that if you come from a highly dysfunctional family that you are destined for failure in life, but as I see it, your cards are stacked higher against your efforts to excel. I say that because in a lot of cases, what one sees, they believe, and the media plays a role in the criminalization of the Black man. When images of Black men are plastered throughout television as thugs, gangsters, and pimps, society develops an image of a Black man being as such, and many cultures absorb that as reality. This unconscious absorption penetrates the subconscious of children and adults. If a child does not have people in their life to counter that misconception, it could penetrate more into that child's mind on into adulthood. There must be positive people in our children's lives and community to counter the labeling.

Everyone's journey is different, and it helps to shape how we are as men. I am a firm believer that the older you get, the more of a story you should have to tell. Below are stories of Black men who came from various backgrounds. They shared who they looked up to, their function in life, and what they are teaching their children. They also discussed what life is like living in America as a Black man. Their stories are thought-provoking.

Growing Up in the 1950s

Gary's Story

Gary grew up at a time in the 1950s where everyone in his neighborhood was part of the community. He grew up in a two-parent home with five brothers and three sisters and attended segregated schools. His teachers cared and were an extension of his family. While racism was prevalent at that time, he didn't know much about it until he was older. His parents did not necessarily tell him about racism, but through their rearing of him, they instructed him what to do and not do. If he did not follow their instructions, he would get a whooping. For example, his father would tell him to keep his mouth shut while out in public.

His father was very instrumental to him and the rock in his family. It was not until later when he fully understood why his father nurtured and instructed him the way he did. He viewed his father as radical and community-oriented. His father and mother both created and were in groups that were about the advancement of the Black community. He received a lot of love from various Black men in the community. For instance, Louis, his mentor, would help him by teaching him about life, making him conscious of himself, and connecting the dots with why his father did what he was doing.

Jobs were limited for Blacks, and his father could never keep a job because he always stood up for himself and would speak out against wrongdoing. He had a gift for barbequing, and because he knew he had to feed his family, he would sell barbeque to make money. His barbeque was considered so good by so many that he started his business on 15th Street and Broadway. His business was very profitable and was once called the "Best Barbeque" in the Louisville community. Gary took over the company in the 1980s. He feels during that time that Black businesses and communities supported each other more because of how Black Americans were treated unfairly.

Gary feels racism was prevalent while growing up and feels it still exists today. The only difference from now and then is that technology allows people to see what is going on. To change what is happening, he believes we have to stand up for what is right and increase awareness. We also must be conscious and know what is going on in this society.

Growing Up in a Two-Parent Home

William's Story

William was born in a middle-class two-parent home in Indianapolis, Indiana. He attended township schools. His father was a great provider to him and the family. He also had several positive role models in his life. Along with his father, his Uncle Dwight stressed to him the value of getting an education and pushing for a better life. His pastor instilled competitiveness, and Rufus, a business owner, taught him about business, having integrity, and the importance of a good work ethic.

While growing up, William saw first-hand how the dynamics of relationships function with his father and mother and used it as a model in his relationships. He has never been married and has two young adult children. They are in college and he feels he has good relationships with them. At one point, his relationship with his children could have been stronger, but even with its challenges, he continued to build the relationship with them by improving communication with them.

William passed down to his son that everyone is not his friend, and he needs to work harder than his counterparts to keep pace. The example he used was explaining to his son about playing baseball and the challenges he experienced. There were times when he was just as good or slightly better than his white counterparts, but they got the starting positions. Therefore, to be better than everyone else, he said he must work harder in everything that he does.

Danny's Story

Danny was born in Owensboro, Kentucky, then moved to Louisville, Kentucky, when he was five years old. He was raised by both his parents and attended private Catholic schools from grades 1 to 12. Even though he attended Catholic school, he felt it did not prepare him better academically. He felt as if he needed Black teachers in his life while growing up, and that did not occur until he entered college at the University of Louisville. Seeing Black professors inspired him.

While growing up, Danny believed in turning deficits into opportunities and he always looked for ways to supplement his education. This practice carried over into the raising of his children. For example, his daughter attended a low-performing school, but he and his wife provided tutoring and proper oversight in her education, and she excelled academically.

Danny's father was his role model while growing up; he taught him right from wrong. While it sounds elementary, he feels that it is huge in today's society because when he came into the workforce, he found out that several people did not have those shared values. He feels that his father's idea of success was for his children to go to college, graduate, and be more successful than he was in life.

Danny believes there is still racism here in America and sees it as a bad seed waiting for the right condition to sprout. He thinks that given society's current state, racism is growing. To combat it, he feels we must continue to speak out against it within the Black community. He also believes one has to look from within and see what contributes to added dysfunction; he sees broken homes, music that glorifies violence, children that are not receiving the proper guidance. As Danny sees it, when you look at Black murders, many of the children are from a failed situation, i.e., parents who are on drugs and are in prison. We have to turn our situation from the inside out.

Kevin's Story

Kevin grew up in Louisville, Kentucky, in a two-parent home. He is married and a father of two daughters. His upbringing was good, and his father was always in his life. He always had his needs and some of his wants met. His father was firm, and his mother a little more relaxed about rules. He learned from his upbringing that life is not always perfect, and sometimes you have to take risks.

Kevin's role model was his father and older cousin, Bruce, from whom he learned about having a good work ethic and doing the right thing. Even when problems occurred in life, such as his car breaking down, he saw his father still going to work. What he saw in that situation, even when problems happened, was his father finding a way to continue to move forward. His father also taught him how to grill and fish. Grilling and fishing together were times for them to bond and for his father to teach him about life. He learned a great deal through his father's actions.

Kevin felt that America was going in the right direction, but it has regressed today because of all the division and unrest. Because of all the discord, he feels vulnerable and disgusted by how people discriminate against others.

As a father of two daughters, he believes Black women face the same obstacles as Black men. He notes there are many strong Black women and that Black men have not supported them fully. As a father, he teaches his daughters how to be self-sufficient, meaning having a career, maintaining themselves financially and domestically, i.e., paying bills, managing money, and cooking.

Robert's Story

Robert grew up in a two-parent middle-class home in a predominantly Black neighborhood in the 1970s and 1980s. He felt that he had a relatively good upbringing that was fun and disciplined. His father was an educator and basketball coach. His mother was an administrative assistant and model. He looked up to his father and uncles, and also the men in his neighborhood.

Given his father was a state and national winning basketball coach, Robert said he learned many life lessons on the basketball court and in sports. His father taught him that sports are life, meaning the discipline of sports can be applied to anything in life. He also taught him that you eat what you kill, meaning, guns are only used to survive, not to kill humans. What he most admired about his father was what he taught him about taking care of his family. He taught him to hunt and grow food, so he would never go hungry. His father and mother both taught him humility and to always remember where he came from.

As a Black man, he feels that America is a work in progress and that Black men have to jump over the hump to success because some doors have opened. He feels success has affected Black men in a good and bad way. The good is they have made more money, and the bad is that too many have left their wives and families when they became more successful. He feels that Black men need to refocus on their children.

As Black men, he feels we need to dig deeper for answers instead of letting society tell us what is right. From digging deeper for answers, Black men will find the truth and be better able to move forward.

Growing Up in Single-Mother Homes

Ramon's Story

Regardless of your circumstances, if you have positive people who are making positive deposits in your life, it builds a child's confidence and propels that child to achieve goals in life. For instance, Ramon was raised in the Beecher Terrace housing projects by a single mother. He is currently a medical doctor. As he grew older, he developed a relationship with his father. While growing up, Ramon received a lot of love and support from his family. He was always called the "smart one" by his family. By continually being called smart, it gave him the confidence to excel academically.

Ramon never ran away from his past and saw it as a motivator. He even has a brick from the recently demolished housing project from where he grew up as a symbol, as a reminder. At an early age he wanted a different life and set the goal of becoming a doctor. When asked about what Black men he looked up to, he said his four uncles, because no matter what hand they were dealt in life, they always kept it moving by working and taking care of their families.

He recognized early that he was gifted academically, so he utilized his gifts by excelling in high school and college. So, what motivated Ramon to excel academically and go after his goal of becoming a doctor? As a father, he reminds his son that he has to be twice as good to be average in America. He also taught his son to be situationally aware.

Chris's Story

Chris was raised in Lincoln Park in Louisville, Kentucky, in the 1960s and 1970s in a single-parent home, headed by his mother, with one sister and four brothers. Growing up, he lived in a neighborhood where he received nurturing from his extended family, neighbors, teachers, and principal. Within his community, there were rules—checks and balances; one was not to disrespect people without consequence. He had a limited relationship with his father. However, he had many Black men who influenced him. Those men were his grandfather, older male cousins, and eight uncles.

His grandfather and uncles taught him how to work and be resourceful, as they had various professions. His grandfather taught him the value of working efficiently and smarter and not harder, and not to do double work. He also taught him about integrity. In one instance, his grandfather took him to a newspaper bin, and the cost of the paper was 25 cents. While that was the price, he could have taken as many papers as he wanted, but he explained and demonstrated the importance of integrity by only taking the number of papers he paid for. Another strong influence was his older brother, who taught him how to treat women and live life.

By Chris's father not being in his home, he felt there was a void in his life. Early on in his life, he would act out his emotions in anger because of that void. He firmly believes if a man were in the house, his outbursts would have probably stopped at an early stage.

Chris is the father of a son who is an adult. He and his son's mother divorced when his son was a toddler. Through and after the divorce, his son lived with his mother in another state. The distance prevented him from having the everyday interaction with and nurturing of his son which tore away at him. Because of the distance, he felt that his parental oversight was limited, meaning that his son's visitation was limited when he played on sports teams and participated in other events at his new location. To improve their relationship, he would write him a snail mail letter every week for ten years. As his son grew up to be a man, he told him to be careful in having kids, being financially wise, and having a relationship with God. He also taught him how to think for himself and not follow the crowd and how to interact with the police.

Kevin's Story

Kevin has been married for 30 years and he is the father of two children – a boy and a girl. Much of his upbringing came from his mother, aunts, and uncles. As he would say, he had a great extended family because they taught him a lot about being a man. Many of his relatives were married for a long time, and most of them worked together. He did not witness any abusive relationships, nor did he see men disrespecting women. That painted a picture in his head about how men treated women and how couples should interact with one another. His views of those relationships did not minimize the challenges couples had; it just highlighted that couples were committed to making it through the tough times together.

While Kevin's father was a part of his life, he thinks the relationship could have been better. His mother and father were not together as a couple, and his mother never spoke bad about him. Through her actions, he learned always to be respectful to others. His father was never disrespectful to his mother because he was a gentleman, and he prided himself in carrying himself as one. His father worked a blue-collar job at General Electric. He never owned gym shoes because of how he carried himself, and he would always dress nicely. He would wear his nice clothes to work and change into his work attire, and after work he would change back into his nice clothes. He was always clean. Kevin remembered going into clubs with him, and everyone knew him.

Kevin did not have a bad relationship with his father, but through it, he wanted to be more of an example and more of a man who keeps his word. He aimed to be a man who was about action, and if he said he was going to do something, he would do it. Having a good work ethic was not an option, but a must.

He and his wife raised their children with the same discipline and values, but he acknowledged that he had to raise his son differently as a Black man in America.

In raising his son, he explained the social stereotypes, traps, and injustices that could capture and entangle him. He taught him to avoid having children until he could take care of himself. He tried to instill in his son that if he had children to leave a legacy for them. He also stressed getting an education and valuing it because it opened more doors of opportunity.

Both of Kevin's children are now grown, and while he instilled in them the values and norms of his family, he felt his children had to live their own lives because he had done his part in raising them. "My son knows what he has to do in this society; he is a man now," said Kevin. With that said, he talks to him straight, man-to-man, as a good father and man should do. Kevin believes if you care about the next man and woman and care about your community with pride, the community will grow.

Donnie's Story

Donnie grew up in Southwick in Louisville and classified his upbringing as poor. His father was not around as much as he would have liked, and his mother worked several jobs to support her family. Seeing his mother work so hard profoundly impacted him, because it taught him to value work. He lived with his father for two years in

Atlanta, between 10 and 12 years of age. His father did not have sufficient financial means, so he lived in East Lake Meadows Public Housing. Those experiences taught him that to get ahead in America, you must have money to live.

Donnie's uncle gave him a lot of guidance, as well as Percy Miller (Master P). He looked up to him as he grew up in the housing project and became financially free. That gave Donnie hope, and he paid attention to that. He met Master P a couple of years ago, and he has provided him with a lot of life and financial advice.

Donnie has a son and two daughters. His son died several years ago. While his son was alive, he instilled in him, and his daughters, the value of finances and community. He wanted them to make better choices than he made in life. He also instilled in them a love for music, especially soul music from the 1970s and 1980s. He has a passion for music because when his dad was not around, it was his way to connect to him.

As a Black man, navigating through America has been a challenge because there is little institutional support for African-Americans. He feels that the system is rigged for him not to win because of the lack of institutional support and perceptions in the community. Through it all, he had to search out and find a way to be successful. While working in corporate America, he made mistakes, and he did not have many mentors to reach out to for guidance.

He feels that having honest relationships are necessary, and thinks that relationships are critical because each relationship will change you for the better, or worse.

Growing Up in Africa and Moving to the United States

Donatus' Story

Donatus was raised in Ghana, Africa, in a two-parent home. He had three brothers, and they were Catholic. It was strict but relaxed, meaning there were strong family protocols, but he could choose his career. The expectation was for you to represent your family and your community as well, so you did not want to bring shame to your family or community. His community was in both the urban and rural areas, which consisted of his extended family. In Ghana, they did not see color as a distinguishing factor because Black was all they saw.

His role models were his parents, teachers, and business people in the Ghanaian community. His connection to the United States came from his mother attending Spalding University in Louisville, Kentucky. She graduated in 1980. He sees his mother as a trailblazer for attending school in America. In 1997, his mother came back to Louisville and was able to secure him a scholarship.

Before coming to the United States, he lived in London, England. That was a challenging period in his life before he was totally on his own. He then moved to the United States. It gave Donatus added confidence when his father told him, "By you making it in England, I know you would be fine in the United States."

Upon arriving in the United States, he immediately noticed and heard the reference to his race. He heard it in London, England, but it was not as prominent as in Louisville, Kentucky. In addition, he realized life in the United States moved much faster than in Ghana.

Donatus has been married for 15 years and has two sons. It has been a challenge teaching his sons because how he was raised is 180-degrees different. He is strict with his sons and spends a great deal of time on values, excellence, and financial prudence. He adds that he and his wife do some things differently because of his Ghanaian upbringing, strictly culturally. However, they have values that are very much alike – spiritually, ethically, etc.

Even though he is from Ghana and can handle himself, he worries about his sons' safety and welfare in America. He did not have to worry about that in Ghana. He teaches his sons about current events and understanding their rights. He wants his sons to have freedom, but sometimes he has to keep them sheltered. They travel often to give them exposure to the world and not to be defined by their zip code. Growing up, you don't think about being an adult, but becoming a parent changes your perspective on how you live and what you want for your children.

Growing Up in a Military Family

Maurice's Story

Growing up in a military family has given Maurice a worldview that we have much in common as people. He grew up in a two-parent home that was very ordered and disciplined. Thus, he had a variety of experiences learning about world politics and social dynamics. He viewed his father as a leader, and the lessons he learned from him have given him greater appreciation as an adult than as a child. The life lessons were not concrete and were not on demand but were a constant pattern over time. Other Black men that he looked up to he learned from through their social interactions over time.

Maurice experienced racism as a child in the military and as an adult. He feels there is good and bad in all relationships. However, he believes institutional racism exists. The benefit of being in a military family, he says, is that he was not pigeonholed into thinking one way. His family had friends in the military, and they often would participate in social settings together. They had friends who were Black, White, and Hispanic. He feels what added to that was how the support systems were set up. Families became close because often those in the military were deployed. Since his father was often deployed he (his father) always had to be flexible in knowing people because when the orders came in, he had to go. There were no options or negotiations.

Living life as a Black man, he is acutely aware that he could be a target of racial profiling or police brutality, so he tries not to put himself in any compromising positions. As he sees it, he knows that the rules are different in this world. He feels that navigating through life is like journeying through a minefield in a war zone. What has helped him most, in being in tune with what happens in this society and looking at society through a sober lens, is seeing the actual reality.

Maurice is the father of two young men, and he tries to raise them truthfully. For example, he remembers his son being upset because a white girl from his school told him that he could only marry Black women. Since his son not did understand, he had to open the conversation about the different types of social dynamics in this society, how the rules are not necessarily the same, and how one cannot control who one falls in love with. It's not about the color of one's skin, but who respects you. As his sons grow into being teenagers, he is having more conversations about day-to-day encounters and social dynamics.

He feels that opportunities for a Black man are circumstantial, and opportunities are connected to your upbringing. His sons have been exposed to seeing America's first Black President of the United States and they are also around accomplished people. His sons are exposed to many Black professionals, and that is a good thing. The disadvantage is that his sons are witnessing the finished product and do not see the work that is going on behind the scenes. They do not clearly understand what it takes to accomplish that level of achievement, thus not knowing how to handle adversity.

As Black men he feels there is always room for improvement and that we owe our women, sons and daughters to be better role models. He feels we as men need to be better controllers of our destiny. We should create different income streams and be intentional in how we interact with others in the workplace. We need to do more mentoring and serve as role models for young Black men.

Growing Up in Rural America

Ed's Story

Ed grew up in Georgetown, Kentucky in a two-parent home; he has two sons and a daughter. As a youth, he was taught that the father was the head of the household; he made the final decision of the house, and that his authority was unquestioned. His father was an authoritative figure, and everything he taught Ed was a teachable moment. There always was teaching in his lessons. In his neighborhood and community of Georgetown, Ed played with kids of all races. His family also had a farm and on the farm were chores that he had to complete. He did not have the liberty to choose what type of chores to complete because he did what he was told to do. Having chores, coupled with the teachings from his parents, instilled in him a strong work ethic, responsibility, and integrity.

While growing up, Ed was aware of racial issues taught to him by his parents. His parents grew up in the Civil Rights and Jim Crow eras, and during that time Blacks had to go to the back of restaurants to receive service. Because of that, his father never ate out. He also taught him not to tell people all his business because it could be used against him.

Because he worked in farming and agriculture, many of the people he worked with were Caucasian. He did not experience a great deal of racial opposition because he either did not see it or because he was isolated from it.

While attending the University of Kentucky and majoring in agriculture, he was one of four African-Americans in the College of Agriculture. During his time there in the 1980s and early 1990s, he did not have any problems. Ed did not experience racism until he graduated from college. In his first career job in Maysville, Kentucky, he was working in the office and a white woman came in. She looked around and asked if everyone worked there. He said, "Yes, how may I help you." She replied, "There is no one else around here and I am sure you would not be able to help me. You must be the janitor."

Ed understands there are racial issues in America, and even his son has experienced racism while playing sports. What happened to his son took him back to when he played sports in high school. He explained if a person called him a racial slur, his Black and white teammates would have defended him because they were a team. To combat racism, he has taught his son to stand up to correct it.

As Black men, Ed feels we need to do more in terms of being fathers to our children. He feels there needs to be more mentoring to young black males because many of them are raised in homes that do not have a father. Because of that, they need some added assistance in navigating through society.

CHAPTER 7: Being the Master of Your Fate and the Captain of Your Soul

In life, there are words of affirmation and poems that build and inspire us to continue to press on. One of my favorite poems is *"Invictus,"* **by William Ernest Henley.** His poem states,

Out of the night that covers me
Black as the pit from pole to pole,
I thank whatever gods maybe
For my unconquerable soul.

In the fell clutch of circumstance,
I have not winced nor cried aloud.
Under the bludgeonings of chance
My head is bloody, but unbowed.

Beyond this place of wrath and tears
Looms but the Horror of the shade,
And yet the menace of the years
Finds, and shall find, me unafraid.
It matters not how strait the gate,
How charged with punishments the scroll,
I am the master of my fate:
I am the captain of my soul.

What resonated with me was, "I am the master of my fate; I am the captain of my soul." That stuck with me because of being the man that I am, and knowing and believing who I am as the master of my fate and the captain of my soul, that is, working in God's plan for my life. Many years have passed since I read this poem, and I believe that if there is a goal that I want to accomplish, I can achieve it. And you ask, "But how can I achieve all my goals, as a Black man in America, when I know the landscape of America?" My answer is you can accomplish anything in this world regardless of who you are, if you have faith and believe in what you are seeking. No one can absolutely hold you back in this society except yourself. Therefore, if you have a dream, put a plan to it. From there, set goals for accomplishing it, then work your plan of execution. To put your dream in place effectively you must be able to execute your dream strategically, meaning, you must know where you live, where you are, who you know, and where you want to go. The reality is some places have more closed doors of opportunity than other places in America. Therefore, being a Black man in America and going after your goals is like playing a game of chess. It is a game because you have many forces coming against you, and you must anticipate your winning moves. One of the leading forces we must see and tackle is racism. Racism is still connected through present-day occurrences; it is ubiquitous. It is on our jobs and in everyday walks of life. It is driving while Black and being stopped just because we are Black. In any event, police brutality could occur that could end in an unnecessary abuse or killing.

My Mom always taught me, what God has for you, no one can take away from you!

To dig deeper into others' minds, I interviewed a group of African-American men about racism and their careers. More than 62 percent of those surveyed felt that racism affected their career growth. Moreover, 83 percent felt that in their career or job they were either targeted or scrutinized unfairly as a Black man. When they encountered a run-in with the police and racism, more than 62 percent said that they would bring awareness to it by speaking up; 35 percent said that they tackled the issue head-on.

Racism is a reality that America must face. America's historical and present-day discrimination and racism dominate the news cycle because of the recent murders of George Floyd in Minneapolis, MN, Ahmaud Arbery in Glynn County, GA, and Brianna Taylor in Louisville, KY. George Floyd's death was the tipping point for many citizens, both Black and white, to become outraged at the criminal justice system. George Floyd was murdered by a police officer, holding his knee on his neck for more than nine minutes. What has people enraged is how the police officer kept his knee on his neck while others were pleading for him to stop, and while George Floyd gasping that he could not breathe, desperately calling out for his mother. To view the video is very painful. It documents his death as evidence of a stubborn continuation of historical and present-day racism in America. These actions have been going on since Black Africans were brought here in 1619 as enslaved persons.

I do not think that racism will end in my lifetime, and in some instances, we cannot control it. However, we must not let it stop us from fulfilling our purpose and achieving our goals in life!

As Black Americans, we must face the reality that racism is real and part of the American fabric. We must continue to fight against the injustices that occur by voting and getting in position to create change. It's also up to our community to create change for ourselves by being the masters of our fate and the captains of our souls. No one is going to control my thoughts, my emotions and liberties. My forefathers fought for our rights, and even though life is not fair at times, we must continue to fight in creating fairness for ourselves.

Because of the constant overt and covert racism in the United States, many Black Americans are questioning whether they are the captains of their faith or the masters of their souls. As a Black man raised here in the United States, I find it a challenge and a test of my will and faith. Black Americans have been taught they have to run two to three times faster to be on pace with their white counterparts. Even though the playing field is not level, I am optimistic that things will change if we continue to fight for what is right.

George Floyd's killing has opened the conversation about Black Americans being compensated through reparations and access to capital as well as elimination of health disparities, housing inequities, and police brutality. Some of our white brothers and sisters in business and corporations acknowledged the unjust treatment and inequities of Black Americans, and companies have placed processes and corrective actions in place to bring about more equity for Black Americans in the workplace. There also has been proposed legislation to change the practices of policing throughout America. While I have seen some new company and governmental policy proposals, we still have a long way to go in righting the wrong of historical slavery in present-day racism.

The United States is considered a democracy. Democracy means that the people should govern. The democracy in which we live has benefited primarily whites more than African-Americans. Because the United States is a democracy, people have historically and presently voted for what changes should occur and how this country should run. This democratic system has been used to legally enslave Black Americans and treat them as second-class citizens, and looked upon as property. At one time Black Americans could not vote, and after the Compromise of 1877, many states instituted racist measures to keep their knees on their necks. Black Americans were lynched, murdered, subjected to pole taxes and were administered a literacy test in order to vote. Their white counterparts did not have to go through this; they only had to register to vote.

Many of these laws to disenfranchise Black Americans were torn down in the 1950s and 1960s through the civil rights movement and by the civil rights leader Thurgood Marshall. Thurgood Marshall and the National Association for the Advancement of Colored People (NAACP) used the landmark *Plessy v. Ferguson* ruling to open many doors for Black Americans. *Plessy v. Ferguson* is the separate-but-equal law. It was set up so that whites and Blacks could have separate accommodations and still carry on in society. Thurgood Marshall and the NAACP knew Black Americans had not been treated equal to their white counterparts, so they attacked the law to win many other cases. The landmark case was the *Brown v. Board of Education* of Topeka, Kansas, in 1954. In this case, the Supreme Court ruled unanimously that children's racial segregation in public schools was unconstitutional. It was one of the decisive steps of progress for Black Americans.

Since 1954, there have been some victories for Black Americans. More job, business, and housing opportunities opened for Black Americans. While there has been progress, there is still a long way to go in leveling the playing field. To level the playing field, there is a need for reparations.

I am a firm believer in reparations for all Black Americans because of slavery and the historical and present-day effects of it. What has and still is happening is the continuous chain-linked fence that cripples the Black community. That chain-linked fence spreads from slavery, lynchings, killings, federally backed programs to limit opportunities, Jim Crow laws, war-on-crime laws, redlining laws and many more. Because of the negative impact of policies on black communities, there must be new policies, systems, and investments to shape our world so that liberty and justice may, in reality, be for all.

Shaping My World According to My Likeness

Your personality, social upbringing and spiritual foundation contribute to your outlook on life. Your makeup sometimes determines your action, and thus life can be a riddle or a puzzle that we all must solve. Figuring out life sometimes requires more work for some than for others. For example, some people know what they would like to be in life at an early age, while others figure it out later. In either case, it does not necessarily mean that one is running faster than the other; it is a matter of coming into our awareness at the right time. It is truly a blessing when one discovers their purpose. What is sad is when one never recognizes their true potential and purpose in life. For example, when I was listening to the *Tom Joyner Morning Show* the Reverend Al Sharpton gave a commentary on life. In his comments, he said one of the most difficult things for a minister to do is to eulogize someone who did not have any purpose in life. I agree with him, because we are all born with a purpose regardless of our circumstances or how society labels us, and it is up to us to manifest that purpose.

Determining who you are and what you want to be in life is totally up to your will and drive to achieve it. Ultimately, circumstances do not have the last say. The truth of the matter is this: society, outside of your family and friends, does not care if you make it in life or not. It is just like when traveling through my neighborhood, and I run into people I have known since I was a young man. Unfortunately, some of them are doing the same things today that they were doing 40 years ago, hanging out in the park and getting full of beer, liquor, and whatever else. I understand that we all have a different chemical makeup. There are substance-abuse problems and mental health issues, and it is my prayer that people would get help if they do have those problems. I also have talked to various people in my community, and from our conversations, I can tell they have given up on life, for various reasons.

Whatever the case, I believe in prayer, and that God can change things. But you must believe that God can change things, and you must believe in yourself.

Regardless of your social or economic status, you will incur some unwanted challenges just because you are a Black man. I say that because many negative stereotypes have labeled us. It is also a matter of gaining economic leverage in this society. While many of us have been educated and have made some economic progress, we still do not have a strong enough economic foundation to be solely independent, to speak up and make decisions to reshape society. This lack of economic foundation and influence carries over into our psyche as men. It affects our mental health and self-worth. So how do you turn around or redirect the direction we as Black men are going?

Further, how do we live in our purpose given the societal challenges? Below are some steps to take in redirecting and empowering who we should be as men. After first praying, the steps are: operating in faith and focus, recognizing when you are unstable, cleaning up what you messed up, redirecting your thinking, having a Plan A, B, and C, learning how to make money independently, investing in yourself and your family, and knowing how to achieve, even when the cards are stacked against you.

Operating in Faith and Focus

The journey of life can be a straightforward path or an enigma, and the reality is we might not understand some things until later. I am a man of God and faith, and I know when I pray for something from God, the answer might be immediate, shortly after that, or later in life. It also might not happen when I anticipate because it might not yet align with God's timing. We know that God's time is always the right time, meaning, it occurs right on time, given our needs and circumstances. In many instances, we might not understand why life's challenges happen at a particular time, only to receive later in life the full understanding. For example, my father told me when he moved to Louisville he applied for job after job without getting hired, and at that time he did not understand why he was not getting hired. He finally took a job as a custodian at Kosair Children's Hospital. After being in that position, he later moved into the technician position, making and fitting people with braces. He then moved into the position of manager of the brace shop, and later to Director of Orthotics and Prosthetics in 1977. He had more than a 40-year career within the same organization. As we spoke one day, he told me the jobs he had applied to years back were all gone due to closing or leaving town, and it became clear to him that the Lord had bigger plans for him. Did he have challenges while working there? Yes, but the Lord protected him and shined a light on his path as he rose through the ranks.

Indeed, overcoming challenges in life helps you to learn, appreciate, and possibly change your trajectory. Regardless of the enormity of challenges, you must work around them to accomplish your goals. You cannot just stop. You might pause or take a detour, but stopping is not an option. Depending on your circumstances, whether you're raising a family and/or facing unemployment, you must do what you can do momentarily to continue with life, including taking odd jobs to put food on the table. I once faced multiple challenges at once and had to work three jobs to keep my house running. Did I like it? Not necessarily, but I knew it was only temporary. While you are in transition, you must never forget your goals, as you continue to work to support yourself and others. One of my uncles dreamed of designing and building homes, but he had a family to support. So, daily, he worked his full-time job, and after work he worked on his dream of becoming a builder. Eventually, he built up his business to the point where he retired from his full-time job and focused solely on his company. When asked about how he did it, he said it was nothing but God that provided for him, along with hard work.

As a man, the more responsibilities you acquire and create in your life, the more you must be responsible.

Both of my children are in college, and I know that they will face many temptations while they gain more independence. Often, I speak to them about staying focused and doing the right thing, not being tempted or making inappropriate decisions because getting caught up in those traps could potentially derail their future goals. In essence, countless individuals fall prey to making impulsive, poor decisions, as temptation distracts their focus and frustrates their personal growth. Teen pregnancy is a prime example. Most teenagers do not have the maturity or resources to take care of a baby. So, they rely on their parents to step into the role of caretaker. This is a continuous cycle that creates a ripple effect throughout families.

Having added responsibilities while going after your dream or purpose requires faith and focus. Faith is believing you will accomplish your goals, and focus is staying on task to achieve them. While married, I wanted to pursue my Master of Business

114

Administration degree. I started school in January, and that prior December, my wife and I had twins. Having one child required a lot of time, but two required even more. She and I discussed if I could continue my education and take an active role in raising them, and it was a huge undertaking. I worked full-time and practically every morning fed one child at 2 a.m., and 5 a.m. I would help get them dressed and take them to the daycare every morning since it was right down the street from where I worked. I had class two days a week, but functioning with a lack of sleep got the best of me. We also took turns watching them as both of us would need breathers occasionally. While it was an adjustment, I knew that it would not last forever, and it did not. I would not trade it for the world because it allowed me time to bond with my children.

I am a firm believer that the Lord will provide even when you think you have to rise to a certain level to compete, and this occurred while I was going through my divorce. I am an advocate for education and love being in the college classroom, teaching and empowering students. Because of my love for the classroom, I wanted to complete my Ph.D. in Business. The opportunity positioned me to meet with some of the top schools in the United States through the Ph.D. Project. The Ph.D. Project is a program in which talented individuals pursue their doctorates in business. The goal was to increase the representation of minorities in business schools. It was an excellent opportunity to provide me with an expense-paid trip to meet with the top universities in business. I applied and was accepted. I was jubilant, but that jubilation soon turned into me assessing the wisdom of just leaving.

At that time, several universities wanted their students to be full-time students because they wanted students to concentrate totally on the program. I had to decide whether to go away to pursue my Ph.D. or be there to support my children. My spirit told me to be there for them, so I decided not to attend the program. While I thought it was a roadblock at the time, the Lord still opened doors for me to teach at the college level, and currently, I am still doing just that.

Recognizing When You Are Unstable

In Scripture, James 1:8 states, "A double-minded man is unstable in all his ways." What does that mean? It means if your mind and heart are divided between the Lord and the world, your habits and actions will be unstable. Who you marry, where you work, the people who are your friends, and your attitude all help to determine your stability.

Being connected to God gives you assurance of stability and guidance.

When you have stability and spiritual guidance, you will be prone to make better decisions, mainly because your God-informed spirit will lead you in the right direction. When you're connected and you know that you're doing something that's not right or if you're going down the wrong path, God will place warning signs in front of you to show you not to go that way. I must admit it's hard to take heed to warning signs because sometimes we want what we want, and we want it right now. For example, we might want to make a lot of money quickly, but the best way to make money might be to get a trade or education, then work our way up into a company or start a business. But because we want money quickly, we might resort to doing things such as selling drugs or other illegal activities. Some of us, even while working a job, might sell drugs on the side. I unequivocally am against selling drugs because it destroys communities and the person who is selling them.

Sometimes in life we could be doing wrong and go down that wrong path so often it becomes our normal. How do you know when you are off-balance, and what are the signs? Answering the question is complex, since we are individuals living in different situations. Below are signs or actions that could take you off balance:

1. **Not thinking independently.** You do not think independently and allow others to control your thoughts and actions. Being able to think independently does not mean that you should be narcissistic. It means that you should have

116

the wherewithal of knowing what you need as a man without allowing anyone to coerce or dictate the path you should go down. Examples of this are people talking you into not opening a business when you want to, or letting someone talk you into buying a purple suit when you know that you need a black suit.

2. **Not knowing where you are going in life.** As we grow up, life should be a building block where we learn what to do and not do. As I grew older, I believed I should be able to look back five years, for example, and be in a better place knowing who I am. If you do not know where you're going in life you will be susceptible to making huge errors and running in circles. Knowing what you want to be and where you want to go as early as possible can pay dividends.

3. **Not standing up when you need to stand up.** Do you know what to stand for in life? As humans, it is only natural for us to have likes and dislikes. For example, as simple as this may be, I do not like mayonnaise, and everybody in my family knows it. You cannot get me to eat any mayonnaise at any cost. While this is minor in the grand scope of things, knowing what you like and stand for plays an essential part in who you are as a man. Alexander Hamilton stated, "If you don't stand for something, you'll fall for anything." Start listing things that you stand for and would not stand for.

4. **Being the first to jump ship.** When something doesn't go your way is your first reaction to jump ship? In life the reality is nothing is always going to go our way, and sometimes adversity or failure can be one of the greatest learning moments as it builds our character and direction. Whether it is a relationship or a job, jumping ship at the first chance of something not going your way is not a good move because it shows that you do not know how to work through adversity toward a solution, whether it's small or large. In most situations, when dealing with some form of adversity, it is best to take a step back and assess the situation. Mind you, some situations require thinking about more quickly than

others, but a knee-jerk reaction might not be the best course of action.

5. **Matters beyond our control.** A mental or physical health issue: I am not a licensed mental health or medical professional, but I know that mental and physical sickness can affect us in several ways, so I will say, please get help.

Working to be stable as a man is a continual process. It's like working to be healthy, and to do so, you have to eat right and exercise. Because we are all different, there are various ways to get to our own level of stability. Reading and meditating on the scriptures and riding my bike are ways that I maintain my stability. Doing so helps me keep a clear mind, an open heart, and a spirit that is at peace.

Clean Up What You Messed Up

As a young man, the brotherhood at the church I attended would frequently sing lyrics from a popular Canton Spirituals song: "Clean up what I messed up, I'm starting my life over again." We all have made mistakes. Some of those mistakes might be minor and others might be severely consequential. There is always another chance to correct your mistakes. As a man, I have made mistakes in relationships, on my job and as a father. As I see it, when we make mistakes, what is important is that we learn from them, and even more, that we are man enough to apologize. For example, I was a manager at a job, and I failed to report an incident to the right point person. Because of that error, I faced suspension. Being discouraged from the incident, I did not know where to turn or how to handle it. I spoke to my mother about this issue, and she said to me, "Alan, just apologize if it was an honest mistake." I followed her direction, and when I met with upper management, I did just that. By apologizing, it changed the whole situation, and I received a warning. I did not get suspended, even more, upper management acknowledged me for being truthful, and I believe that added more respect for who I am.

Today, we rarely see people stand up and acknowledge any errors or wrongdoing. They continuously place the blame on others and sometimes, when they do get caught, they might apologize. In addition, they dig themselves further into a hole by blaming others and lying. That is not the way to operate. I believe that you should exercise prudence in knowing when to speak up and when to be quiet because a sharp tongue could do more harm than good. So how do you clean up what you *do* mess up? Below are some suggestions, and I already know this list could be endless:

1. **Think about the consequences before acting.** This applies if you are married and are thinking about stepping out on your husband or wife; working a job and thinking about stealing something, or if you're a father not supporting your children. All of those situations could have a profound impact. If you step out on your husband or wife, you could risk damaging your marriage or, even more, getting physically hurt. If you steal from a job, for example, you could risk being fired or possibly going to jail. If you are not the mother or father you should be to your children, you risk having the disconnection and disrespect from your children; equally important, your children could grow older being less than they should be, and emotionally broken.

2. **Pray for strength, guidance, and for the Lord to build a fence around you.** Back in the 1990s, P Diddy and Mase came out with a song called, "Mo Money, Mo Problems." Yes, like the prodigal son in the Bible, when you have money, you are more likely to have friends, both real and fake. Often, if you are a man with money, you become even more attractive to women, and those trappings could affect you emotionally and financially. The attraction sometimes could be real or false. Regardless, you must keep your eyes open and practice a level of discernment. I believe if people are not right, time will expose them.

3. **When you mess up, apologize, and change your ways.** I have said to several people that I can show you better than I can tell you. What I mean by that is my actions always speak

more effectively than words. When you do mess up, the consequences could mean closure, such as a divorce from your significant other or termination from a job. In either case, do not continue doing what you did that caused you to mess up in the first place. Doing that only shows that you are not remorseful and that you did not learn from your errors.

Cleaning up what you messed up requires you to look in the mirror and ask who you are, what consequences you caused, and how you can correct it. This requires courage as many of us cannot handle looking in the mirror at the truth. If you genuinely want to clean up what you messed up, you must stand up and be a man about it.

Redirecting Your Thinking

Early on in life, I came across this poem called "The Man Who Thinks He Can" by Walter D. Wintle. It states,

If you think you are beaten, you are;
If you think you dare not, you don't;
If you'd like to win, but think you can't,
It's almost a cinch that you won't.
If you think you'll lose, you're lost,
For out in the world, we find
Success begins with a fellow's will,
It's all in the state of mind.

If you think you're outcasted, you are;
You've got to think high to rise.
You've got to be sure of yourself before
You can ever win a prize.
Life's battles don't always go
To the stronger or faster man;
But sooner or later, the man who wins
Is the one who thinks he can.

This poem has many meanings because of how we see ourselves and what we believe will occur in our journey. I am a big football fan, and my brother Ray and I often watched games together. When we were not together we would call to discuss the games. During those discussions he would say it was about what was going on between their ears. That determined whether they rose to the occasion, or not. He meant that if one had a winning mentality, they would never give up winning. I agreed with him, because in reflecting on when I played football in high school, I could sense when we were mentally focused or not in games. There were times when we wanted to win games more than others, and in those games, we fought like hell to win. In other games, we did not exhibit as much effort, and we did not fight as much. It had to do with how we prepared, who we were playing, and how we were feeling from injuries.

Equating how we perform in games to how we sometimes perform in life, we will have situations that might hamper our spirit to continue the fight to win. So how do you put out a great effort to achieve what you want? It all starts with you! It's like when Muhammad Ali would shout, "I'm the greatest!" He did not shout that just to be shouting it; he shouted that because he believed in himself, and the reason why he thought it was because he worked harder than anyone else. Relatives that went to school with him told me that in the mornings when they caught the bus, instead of riding the bus, Muhammad Ali would run to school. Muhammad Ali believed he was the greatest because he put the work in, he had faith, and he focused on his goals. Below are strategies for redirecting your thinking.

1. **Write words of affirmation about your goals in life and do the work.** Words of affirmation are positive reinforcements to the mind, body, and soul! However, reciting words of affirmation and not doing anything will not get you closer to achieving your goals; they are only words you are reading. Write out the words of affirmation, and after mapping out a strategy, work on your goals. After developing your goals, lay out a strategy of execution.

2. **Select your friends and confidants wisely.** I believe in respecting everyone because of my upbringing. Respecting people is a core belief I carry in my personal and professional life. While I respect everyone, I know we are all different. Because of that, I know that some people are equipped to give me wise counsel while others are not. Align your goals with people who have experience in the areas where you are seeking to go. These people will better assist you and give you reliable information in terms of what you need to do to accomplish your goals.

3. **Come to your conclusion by researching it, not by hearing it.** People who know me know that I am reserved and do not have much to say. Often, I listen to what others are saying, and sometimes I process what they are saying before responding too quickly or not knowing what I am talking about. That is why I do a lot of research to determine my conclusions. I'm not saying that I do not believe people, but I want to underscore that I am an independent thinker, meaning, people just can't tell me anything and expect me to believe it.

Redirecting your thinking requires a shift in your habits and outlook on life. Like anything we do, it involves repetition for it to become habit-forming. Once it becomes habit-forming, you may then unconsciously act out how you align your thinking to be independent and productive.

Always have a Plan A, B, and C, but Pray and Seek Guidance First!

There are only two guarantees in life: you must pay taxes, and you must die one day. With that said, nothing else is guaranteed, no matter what we invest in or acquire. When I asked an administrator at the University of Louisville while earning my Master in Public Administration degree, what guarantees do I have by obtaining this degree? His reply was, "Having this degree and not knowing anybody would be as valuable as twenty-five cents in your pocket." He was saying that I must know people who can speak on my behalf. I also heard him say that I must have a plan.

The perceived historical pattern for African-Americans in the job market, whether true or untrue, is that we are the last hired and the first fired. If that is a constant pattern, you have to prepare yourself to sustain your standard of living by taking care of yourself and family. You must have a plan, and to solidify it, I believe it is a must to first pray to God for guidance. My mother always taught me what God intends for you, no man can take away from you. I believe that wholeheartedly.

Because of the dynamics of life, if you have a job, I recommend that you learn every aspect of the job and what benefits your job has to offer. I say that because I believe every job you have in life is a building block that helps to shape and build onto who you are; therefore, absorbing what is offered is essential. I also recommend that you create different streams of income from it, which requires sacrificing and moving prudently on investment opportunities such as acquiring an investment property, starting a side business, or investing in the stock market. You cannot put all your eggs in one basket, and if you spend all of your money, you will find yourself in the poorhouse and being enslaved to others. How do you create and execute plans A, B, and C?

- Do a self-assessment of your skills and your passion.

- Determine how much it would cost, resources needed, the level of risk and how long it would take to reach your goals for all three plans.

- If you are in a relationship or marriage, make sure to communicate your plans with your partner. That is essential because she could add value and support to your plans.

- Develop a strategy and take steps of execution in your first plan (Plan A) and so forth.

In this life you are not always going to get what you want. That is why you must have plans in place, and having back-up plans in place may lessen some of your setbacks.

Learn How to Make Money Independently!

The unemployment rate for black men is the highest among all groups in the United States. Why is that so? Is it because we are not educated or skilled, or is it because we are lazy? All three of those questions do not hold merit as to why Black men have the highest unemployment rate. Many will say it is because of systemic racism and the negative stereotypes that black men are labeled with in this society. While I am a firm believer in carving out your own path and not carrying the weight of racism on your shoulders, I know that systemic racism is present in this society and probably will be when I die.

It would be challenging to change all the hearts of people who think differently from me. So, we have to fight against racism and work around it. If it is affecting me directly, I must stand up for what is right. We also must recognize when we need to pivot to work around it to continue achieving our goals. Having the wherewithal for knowing how to combat racism and knowing when to pivot requires a level of prudence and faith. There will be times when you must tackle racism head-on and other times when you need to make strategic moves to seek and move to other opportunities. Whatever the case may be, you have to focus on your livelihood and sustainability. That requires you to not only look at your current situation, but also the future.

Before the 1960s and integration, there were more Black-owned businesses, and the dollar circulated more in Black communities. There were black-owned funeral homes, insurance companies, and banks because white-owned companies would not service the Black community. While these businesses existed, their financial positions and ability to obtain capital were nowhere near those of white businesses. Because of inequality, there was a push for integration and equal access to capital. As integration evolved, Black businesses became scattered, and the Black dollar left the Black community. While some doors of access have opened slightly, Black Americans still fight for higher pay and access equal to their white counterparts.

While the fight must continue, Black Americans also must focus on creating an economic foundation in the Black community.

As Black men, we must change our mindset from being consumers (purchasing from others), to being producers (creating a product or service to be purchased).

One of the reasons why unemployment is so high for Black men is that we, as Black Americans, do not have an economic foundation of businesses and commerce occurring within our communities. By not having an economic foundation and limited access to capital to create businesses, you always have to depend on someone else for resources and livelihood. That forces you to have to answer to and rely on others, which in turn places you in an unsecured level of dependency. I say unsecured because there are no guarantees to the jobs we work. So, to minimize our risk of setbacks, we must increase our independence level by investing more and creating our own businesses and other assets.

Ownership is the key to creating Black wealth. I am not saying that we should not work for anyone, because we built the foundation of America. But Black Americans should be in decision-making roles in corporate endeavors and government. In addition, we are one of the largest consumers of products and services worldwide. As Black Americans, we consume too much, and we are running an astronomical deficit when it comes to being producers—noted by the author and intellectual W.E.B. DuBois, "We've given all of our economic power away. When you owe another, your freedom is impaired." DuBois counseled, "Your ability to decide your destiny is tainted by the amount you owe (Kimbro, 2020)." So how do we make a paradigm shift from being huge consumers to being producers? It requires working together, strengthening our relationships with people, and fighting against inequality. While I am placing the ball in Black America's court to change from being consumers to producers, it is not our total responsibility because of the dynamics of how America operates.

As a business owner, I have witnessed how the power of relationships with banks and the government helps to support and grow businesses. America's landscape has shown me that location and who is in political office matters in terms of how opportunities are distributed to Black businesses. In some cities, the distribution of opportunities goes to just a few Black businesses, and in other places, the distribution is better. For example, in Marion Barry's book, *Mayor for Life*, when he took office as mayor of Washington D.C., African-American businesses were only receiving three percent of prime contracts. Given the Black population was 70 percent in the 1980s, he saw that low percentage as a huge disparity. He worked to change that, and when he left office, 47 percent of prime contracts went to Black-owned businesses. No wonder many Black Americans loved him. As a friend from there told me, "Marion made a lot of Blacks millionaires."

There needs to be better access and greater distribution of capital in establishing the foundation in black communities. Historical and present-day policies have disenfranchised and crippled black communities. These policies began with slavery and continued like a chain-link fence connected to present-day occurrences. There must be a change, and reparations, as I noted earlier, must be awarded to Black Americans.

If you look at how the United States was formed leading up to how Black Americans are treated today, you will understand why reparations are needed. Every group that has been wronged in the United States has received reparations except Black Americans. Some of us do not fully understand the history of the United States and how policies, directly and indirectly, benefited our white counterparts and how they placed the knee on the necks of Black and brown people. Many people don't want to talk about reparations because, in my opinion, they do not fully understand what it means. In addition, they think it is going to affect their pocketbook. Some people say it happened so long ago, so how and why should they be responsible for giving Black Americans reparations? Some would even say if Black Americans receive reparations, they will just go and spend the money on something nonconstructive. My reply to those that discuss what they think will happen with the reparations instead of looking at why there need to be reparations is that you cannot place any group of people in one box. Like any other race, Black Americans are diverse in their intellectual, practical, and spiritual humanity. While the U.S. government owes Black communities and Black Americans reparations, I feel that we cannot wait for that to happen. That's why we need to start today building our own economic foundation.

Invest in Yourself and Your Family

Dr. Joseph McMillan is my fraternity brother and a giant in the Louisville community. He was a professor at the University of Louisville and would host the Black Family Conference annually. His conference highlighted both international, national, and local figures and experts covering various topics for strengthening the family and the community. We would work out at the same place, and he was the type of man you listened to whenever he spoke. While working out in the gym, he gave me, as I would call it, some profound advice. He said to me, "Alan, it is good to be working in the community, but you make sure that you take care of yourself and your family first before putting all of your efforts in the community." While his advice was straightforward and direct, I found it profound and made sure I would be on stable ground. When you're on stable ground, you are better prepared to strengthen and contribute to your community. Moreover, when you have a family and make deposits in your family and children, that creates an even stronger community.

Many of the Black communities are poverty-stricken because of policies and disproportionate investments. When you have that in place, coupled with the high unemployment rate, you're going to have more devastation—people doing drugs and crime, and thus suffer a greater rate of hopelessness. I have to say that the community I grew up in does not look like the same community today. While growing up in West Louisville, many homes had two

127

parents and were owned. Today, there are many abandoned homes in West Louisville and many are rented. Because of those factors, which exists in many urban communities across America, the communities are stained and worn, and they have an unwelcome presence. We, as Black Americans, must change that, and we cannot wait for others to do it for us. To build onto our communities, Black men must start investing in themselves and their families and have sustainable relationships. That would be a step forward in establishing an economic foundation.

CHAPTER 8: Relationships Matter

As a young man, I would hear the old saying, "Behind every successful man is a good woman." While it might not be politically correct to say "behind a man," it is more appropriate to say beside every successful man is a successful woman and vice versa. I say that because relationships are critical to one's upward mobility and sustainability in life. Relationships can be very powerful or very detrimental. They can be powerful when you have two focused individuals who share the same values and desire to build onto their lives. They can also be detrimental when two people operate in discord and disunity. I have said to my son and daughter that they need to be mindful of the relationships they get into because that person could be the wind beneath their wings or the anvil at their ankles—meaning someone could propel you, keep you at a standstill, or even take you down. For that reason, who you have as your mate can dictate your trajectory in life.

The dynamics of relationships have changed over time. There has been a shift in who people date and marry and also who's the breadwinner in a household. The overall commitment to being a team has changed as well. Why a person is attracted to another person sometimes is even against the concept of true love. We love that woman because she is a doctor, or we love that man because he plays in the NFL, both of which produce a financially secure lifestyle. We all are impressed with accomplished people, however, loving a person because of a title or what he/she has amassed creates a false sense of what love truly is. Therefore, a "barometric test" would reveal, if you lost everything, would that person still be in your corner?

Looking back at my parents' relationship, my father was more of the breadwinner, and my mother was the nurturer of the home. My mother eventually got a part-time job after I was born. My father believed that he was to provide for the family, and my mother believed that a man was to take care of her and she would take care of the house. She would say to me when I brought women home that I was interested in, for my family to meet, "These women today just don't know how to cook or take care of the house." I would have to explain to Mom that more women were in the job market, and some women were even the breadwinners of the household. That concept was foreign to her because she grew up in an era where the man provided for the home and family, and women nurtured the children and took care of the house. While I believe the dynamics and roles of relationships have changed over time, one thing that is still constant is that everyone wants and seeks love at some level.

When you talk to women, there is a perception that there is a shortage of good Black men. They would say that black men are either in prison, gay, or cannot be committed to just one woman. While they say that, I do not subscribe to the idea that there is a shortage. When I speak to black men, they believe there are good men out there. When women say there is a shortage, they are saying that they are not meeting the type of men they envisioned having. For example, a woman might want a college-educated man, but he might not be a man she would like. I believe that education does not represent anyone's character and drive to be successful. Still, in today's society, your character can only get you so far in a relationship without having a vision, focus, and love in your heart.

Finding the right mate requires prayer, time, and a spirit of discernment.

More Black women than Black men have amassed educational and financial stability, and some women view having a man in their life who is equal to them and equally yoked is essential. Further, I cannot criticize any woman or man for wanting their mate to bring what they have to the table. It is their right to view what they see as good or bad for them. The reality is, there must be some level of chemistry and commonality for a relationship to have a chance of sustainability. Commonality and chemistry are paramount, because while I feel that I am a good man, I know that I am not a good man for every woman. This means who I am as a man and what I value might not align with what some women want. The same is true for good women that I meet who might not be attractive to me.

What Do Black Women Feel About Their Relationships with Black Men?

To analyze the thoughts and opinions of women, I conducted a focus group survey. This group consisted of women aged 21 and over. The respondents lived in the South, the Midwest, West, and Northeast. Most of the respondents either had a bachelor's are a master's degree. Others received some college or a professional or doctoral degree. The majority of the respondents were single. Twenty percent were divorced, and 19 percent were married. When I asked them to rank what success meant to them, more than 75 percent responded that being healthy, and having peace in their life was extremely important. Forty-four percent said having a successful career and financial options were somewhat important, and 44 percent said having a family and close friends was important. Fifty-six percent said being in a relationship or married to a man was not as important.

When asked to rank what they viewed as success in a Black man, 82 percent said having a God-fearing black man was extremely important. Sixty-seven percent said having stable employment, regardless if it was blue- or white-collar, or self-employed, was very important. Fifty-four percent said Black men having a college degree was not as important, and 57 percent said a Black man in an executive position was not important at all. Forty-eight percent said seeing black men married and having a family was important in terms of success.

When asked about their view of Black men in the United States, 56 percent felt that Black men were criminalized and targeted; 46 percent felt Black men needed to take control of their destiny; and 34 percent assert Black men are a strong force in America.

When asked if they agreed that single-parent households contributed to Black men having higher unemployment rates, unstable relationships, inactive parenting, or a higher incarceration level, 42 percent agreed, and 25 percent strongly agreed those were contributing factors.

When asked about having positive Black role models while growing up, 50 percent of women said they had three or more positive Black male role models, and 21 percent said that they had two male role models in their lives. When asked about Black men's negative stereotypes, and if they believed them, 48 percent said they did not believe it, and 33 percent were not sure.

When I asked women to rank what they respect most about a Black man, more than 89 percent said his spirituality was extremely important, and 84 percent said his intellect was extremely important. Eighty-eight percent said his street knowledge was not as important or not important at all to them. Thirty-eight percent said his masculinity was somewhat important to them. Twenty-eight percent said his hustle-type mentality, that is, always finding a way to be successful, was somewhat important.

When asked what frustrated women most about Black men, 49 percent said his lack of commitment in relationships frustrated them the most. Fifty percent said men's lack of financial resources or money, and 43 percent said his lack of spirituality frustrated them.

In terms of marriage and sustainability, I asked the women if long term marriages (25 years or longer) was a thing of the past; over 56 percent said they did not feel it was a thing of the past, and 29 percent felt it was a thing of the past. When I asked how important it was for them to be in a relationship or married to a black man, 29 percent said it was very important, 28 percent said it was somewhat important, and 21 percent said it was extremely important. Fifteen percent said it was not as important, and seven percent said it was not important. When asked if they felt Black men needed to man up and hold themselves more accountable for their actions, 91 percent of the women said yes, and three percent said no.

Twenty-nine percent of women surveyed agreed that Black women have better career opportunities than black men because of the perception of abuse and stereotypes of black men. Twenty-two percent of the women neither agreed nor disagreed with that assessment. Twelve percent strongly agreed that black women had better career opportunities, and 14 percent somewhat agreed.

When asked why black women felt there are not enough good Black men, 59 percent said there were not enough black men of good character and equally yoked in terms of career, education, and income. Thirty-eight percent of women felt there are not enough black men that could support a family financially. Twenty-nine percent felt there are not enough men that women desire, meaning, a professional athlete, doctor, corporate executive, or attorney. Thirty-eight percent of women felt, as women, they do not know what they want.

What Are the Women Saying About Relationships?

Relationships between men and women have evolved, partly because women have shifted from being more of the home's caretaker to being a force in the job market. That is the case now as more women are in the workforce and are moving through the ranks, becoming executives, and running companies. Even though women's roles have increased in the workplace, they still play a significant role in the house. That is why one of my supervisors said he believed that women were better managers than men. He felt they could multitask better than men. In his view, women were still taking care of the house and working and still keeping things functional. Even though many women are in the workforce and are rising through the ranks, they still need and desire relationships and marriage. From my survey, most women want to be in a relationship with a Black man, and even though there are strong desires for one, they have challenges finding the right mate. I say the *right mate* because many women can find success in merely entertaining a relationship with a man below her reasonable standards; however, when women say they want the right man, they want to be with a man they are compatible with, able to feel protected by and equally yoked. Being equally yoked, in my view, means that there should be some qualities that match up between the man and the woman. For example, I have certain qualities that I want in a woman, such as being a woman in Christ, being financially prudent, being intellectually astute, and having the ability to communicate. Those are just some of the core qualities that I desire. As a man, I have a wish list—what I would call icing on the cake. I would love to have a woman who loves cycling as I do, but that list is not as important as the core qualities I desire. We all have different attributes that we desire, and rightly so; we all have different needs and wants, regardless of whether you are a man or a woman. Even though we do not see the qualities we desire in a partner, we question if we should continue to pursue that person. It depends on the person and your current circumstance. With that said, the women surveyed clearly stated that they want a man who is God-fearing, has a stable and consistent income, knows where he's going, and is able to hold himself accountable

What Do Black Men Think About Themselves and Their Relationships with Black Women?

After surveying black women, I surveyed Black men. I did this to get a black man's perspective on what was going on in their minds, and to get a better idea of how Black men and women should interact in relationships. By no means am I saying that I should be a marriage counselor, because I have always stated that there are no two relationships that are alike. We are all unique in our way, and in any given situation, that uniqueness could change.

I surveyed men primarily residing in the South and Midwest, with a few living in the West and Northeast. The majority of the men surveyed were between the ages of 21 and older, married, with either a bachelor's or master's degree. Twenty-nine percent had three or more children, with 26 percent having two children. Twenty-seven percent did not have any children. Of those with children, 52 percent said their children were by one woman, and 17 percent said their children were by two different women. Fifty-three percent said they had a great relationship with their children, and 31 percent said they had a good relationship with them. Eight percent said their relationship could be better, and two percent did not have relationships with their children. Forty percent of the men with children had children 21 years of age and above, and 21 percent had children between 16 and 21. Twenty-five percent had children between the ages of one and 10.

Contrary to societal stereotypes, 61 percent of the men surveyed grew up in a two-parent home, while 32 percent grew up in a single-parent home headed by their mother. Two percent grew up in a single-parent home headed by their father. When I asked these men to classify their upbringing, 50 percent said they had a good upbringing regarding having all needs and wants met, meaning they had food, shelter, medical care, clothes, and material items. Thirty-eight percent said they had a great upbringing by having all their needs and wants met. In terms of Black male role models in their life, 58 percent said their fathers were their role models, and 50 percent said that a family member, such as a brother or uncle, was their role model. Thirty-five percent said either a teacher, coach, or neighbor was their role model, and 21 percent said their pastor was their role model.

Sixty-one percent surveyed felt they were successful, and only two percent felt that they were not, while 38 percent felt they were still working on achieving success. When asked what success looked like to them; 86 percent said being healthy mentally, emotionally, and physically was a sign of success, and 68 percent said being financially secure was a sign of success. Sixty-four percent said being connected to God is a sign of success, and 41 percent said having the right woman in their life is a sign of success.

When asked what drove them to achieve, 80 percent said their goals in life, 62 percent said that achievement was instilled in them by their parents; and 58 percent said having personal responsibilities, such as having a wife and family, drove them to achieve. Thirty-two percent said the fear of failure drove them to achieve, and 29 percent said they wanted to reverse how they grew up. Three percent said obtaining material possessions, and two percent said they did not know how to be successful.

When asked if they felt like racism has affected their career growth, 62 percent said yes, and 26 percent said no. Fifty-five percent said racism played a role in their life. Thirty-five percent somewhat agreed they were targeted and scrutinized unfairly as Black men in their career positions. Forty-eight percent either agreed or strongly agreed they were unfairly targeted on their jobs, and 12 percent were not sure about being unfairly targeted.

When asked how they handled racism in life, 62 percent said that they would bring up awareness about it by speaking up, 35 percent would tackle it head-on to stop it, and 33 percent said that depending on the level of racism, they may speak up. Thirty-five percent said they would pray about it, and 26 percent said they would take a step back and think of a strategy to change it.

Eighty-nine percent of the Black men surveyed felt they could accomplish anything, and if they failed, 82 percent said they would gather their thoughts and turn their failures into opportunities. Seventy-five percent said they would work harder to minimize their failures.

Seventy-four percent felt they controlled their destiny, and 17 percent felt they did not. Seventy-four percent felt they could achieve millionaire status if they worked hard and invested properly, whereas 38 percent felt they could achieve billionaire status if they worked hard and invested properly. Fifty-three percent strongly agreed that to obtain millionaire status or higher they would need to create their own business instead of working for someone else. Eighty-eight percent felt that a woman played a role in their success.

When asked what they wish they had more of in being prepared for life, 45 percent wished they had a better understanding of their purpose in life. Forty-two percent said they wished they had more education or a trade; 40 percent wished they had more positive Black men in their lives, and 32 percent wished they had more guidance from their fathers.

What Are the Men Saying in the Survey?

Many of the men surveyed had an educational background and a strong black male role model in their lives, whether the modeling came from their father, a family member, or someone from school or church. I raised these two points because when you have a positive Black male role model in a young Black male's life, his chances of going in the right direction become greater. I am not taking anything away from women, but I believe that for a Black male to fully become a man, he must be nurtured by a man.

In addition, even though many of the respondents obtained at least a bachelor's degree, they still experienced racism and negative stereotypes at work, which is not surprising, especially if you are a Black man working in some level of an organization. The scrutiny experienced has been around for centuries, and for change to take place, a changing of the mindset and heart has to occur. We cannot control what is in a person's mind or heart, but we can change where we work and how we accept the scrutiny. What am I saying?

While we cannot change how people feel about Black men, we can change how we respond and the paths we travel.

The dynamics of relationships between a man and woman, or couples, could be complex. I do not personally believe that couples get together or marry just to break up. While there are various motivations why couples marry, I believe some consistent behaviors must be in alignment for the relationship to work. To recognize those patterns, we must have our emotional and spiritual eyes open. In either case, I believe when love is truly in the equation, people ultimately want the relationship to last.

What Makes Relationships Last?

People are in relationships for various reasons. Some are in relationships for money, love, support, or what Susan, a Black woman who was surveyed says. She added that women fundamentally want to be valued. I do not believe that people get into relationships to break up or to get a divorce; rather, they do not see the holistic picture of the relationship dynamic. There are challenges that occur while dating and during marriages that cause couples to divorce. The top reason couples divorce is money, because paying bills or not being able could cause stress. Other reasons are infidelity, constant arguing, lack of intimacy, and substance abuse. Do these reasons why people divorce just pop up, or do people ignore them before they tie the knot? I believe both can happen in relationships because sometimes we ignore what is right in front of our faces. Relationships do evolve, meaning, circumstances can cause couples to change how they interact with one another. So how do you handle surprises that pop up at the beginning of a marriage and navigate through the various challenges? I questioned various people that were married, divorced, and seeking to get married.

Maurice, one of the Black men surveyed, believes that transparency and trust need to be established at the beginning of a relationship to minimize any surprises that might pop up while married. For example, telling your mate that you want a child after marriage and never mentioning it while in a relationship could present a challenge. Moreover, he believes that core values are nonnegotiable and should be communicated while in the relationship before marriage.

Susan believes communication is the success and failure of relationships. For example, open communication helps lay the foundation of it, whereas the lack of it creates a misunderstanding of expectations and values. For marriages to last, she believes there must be a foundation that encompasses emotional, spiritual, physical, and mental connections. Couples also must be selfless, must reflect consideration for one another, and must have a vision for the union, insulated with love.

Carl, who has been married for more than 60 years, believes couples need to be equally yoked and have the same interests to a large extent. No one should overrule the other. If they have children, they should not argue in front of them, and they should settle their differences elsewhere. He believes that couples need to be on the same accord with finances, children, and direction in life.

In his first marriage, Donnie acted as if it was merely a relationship instead of a marriage, and it was more about the individual than the couple. In his current marriage, it is more about looking out for each other and being more intentional, focusing on their intentions; they go to a counselor every other month.

Pam believes you first must trust yourself in a relationship, and be honest to make it in a relationship. She also believes in being with a like-minded person. She believes one must be forgiving and open-minded because people are going to make mistakes throughout the marriage.

After 40 years of marriage, Ann thinks the reality is, as couples mature, they find out more about their mate. She believes that coming into a marriage, people have stars in their eyes and high expectations, and as the marriage progresses, they see more about their mate. She does not believe that one is more right or more wrong than the other in a relationship, because the Bible speaks of being as one. She feels that couples need to have agape love, to learn how to love, and to forgive by letting things go. She also believes in open communication, and understands how to agree to disagree, respect one another, and compromise.

If you have lived long enough, I am sure you have stories to tell about the successes, failures, and missed opportunities in relationships. Whatever the case, I hope you learn from each relationship, especially your personal growth in interacting and communicating within a relationship. I believe in relationships and marriage because both are natural occurrences that build onto who you are, and possibly, who you will become.

CHAPTER 9: Creating Our Own Economic Foundation

After graduating from college, I had various career opportunities that were good and bad and built onto my skill set and wisdom. I do not have any regrets, because both the good and bad experiences allowed me to take a step back to evaluate my actions. Part of the evaluation consisted of me asking, "Who is Alan Davis Benson, what does he represent, what are his core values, and where does he want to go?" After prayer, reflection, and coaching I came to a greater awareness of who I was, what I represented, and what was best for me in life. I came into my authentic self and indeed grew to a greater level of peace.

When you are at a level of peace and follow through on changing who you are, you will see yourself more clearly and be better able to capitalize on your skills, talents, and purpose. Your mindset and habits even change. For me, what changed was my outlook and approach to challenges. I shifted my mindset from going out looking for a job to allowing God to use me to capitalize on my talents to create opportunities for myself. I relied on Him to give me the spirit of discernment and rolled up my sleeves and opened my mind to use my intellectual capital according to His will.

When I receive a calling from God to move, that is affirmation that the time is right for me to move. Knowing that God has my back, and that He will provide does not mean I can just sit back and expect blessings to fall from the sky. I must do the work, because faith without works is dead. For example, while I have goals for my business, I must pray, plan, and follow through to achieve my goals. Doing so requires sacrifice, support, and resources. Some might have a treasure chest of money for a business, and some might have to work their day job while growing their business. In either case, there must be a balance and organization between the two to stay on task to achieve your goals.

Your Personal Inventory

If you take an inventory of your life's journey, I am sure there were things you liked and things you disliked. You also know what jobs you excelled in and those you did not excel in. Whether you succeeded or failed at a job, there were some takeaways that added to your skills. Assembling the skills you acquired throughout the years serves as the ladder for you to climb to greater heights. Each skill you learn is an added benefit to you. For example, as a young child, I would shovel snow and cut grass to make money. Along with the physical labor of it, I learned how to negotiate my pricing based on the workload. While in the 12th grade, I started working at the local newspaper selling subscriptions. From that job I learned how to sell. After returning from the Gulf War, I was promoted to Sales Supervisor, and from that position, I learned how to motivate and manage people. After graduating from college, I went into a management program at a bank and learned about budgeting, lending, relationship building, and consumer lending. After earning my first masters, I moved to Lafayette, Indiana and worked as a project manager. In that capacity, I learned project management, community development block grants, and research. After moving back to Louisville, Kentucky, and earning my MBA, I learned about education policy, grant management, profit and loss management. All the skills I acquired helped to make me a knowledgeable and skilled person, and better prepared me to be a business owner.

When you take an inventory of your skills learned throughout life, I am sure you would find some of the skills you use today you probably learned years ago. If you cannot assemble or recall what you have acquired, write down what you are passionate about doing and find easy to accomplish. We all have it in us to do special and great things, so start today! In addition, reflect on the signs you have seen that affirm the direction you should go.

Signs for Creating Your Own

I believe the Holy Spirit places people and signs in your life to give you a nudge, better clarity, and affirmation on the direction you should be going. What reminded me of this again was when I was a manager at Sears Holding Corporation. I met a manager, and we had a conversation about family and life. He told me he had children, and they were out of college and doing quite well, but he said something that burned deep in my soul, and it stayed with me from that time to even now. He said that he taught them to go to college to get a job when he should have taught them to go to college to create a job as well. That made me think about who I was at that time and where I wanted to go. I found it interesting because I had been contemplating starting a business but had not followed through in starting one. Our conversation confirmed that I needed to start a consulting business. I also established some entrepreneurial programs as the president of the National Black MBA Association – Kentucky Chapter. Our programs brought awareness and support for entrepreneurs and those seeking to create their own business. In developing my business, I knew that some things had to happen, such as having a plan, a strategy of execution, resources, connections, and, more importantly, faith. Given that I was new to operating my own business, I wanted to learn as much as possible about running a business, how Black-owned businesses faired in Louisville, Kentucky, and how Black-owned businesses faired in America. Learning about it was, and still is, an eye-opening experience.

Without commitment, you will never start, but more importantly, without consistency, you will never finish. Keep working and striving!

—Denzel Washington

I quickly learned that starting and operating a business was like running a marathon and could easily be tiring, but my faith and determination kept me going. I am one of the many Black American business owners that had the faith and determination to start a business. It was a choice for me to start a business, but my forefathers did not have the choices I have. I would bet starting a business during that time was much more difficult, but that did not stop them.

The History of Black Businesses and The Present-Day Black Economy

While starting a business gives one the opportunity to create wealth, its economic impact could create job opportunities for others, and jobs are one of the main drivers of the United States economy. Our forefathers saw just that, because opportunities for Black Americans were bleak and oppressive. For those reasons, Black Americans have a long history of starting and owning businesses. They started businesses in the 1800s and 1900s because of extremely oppressive conditions and segregation. They saw creating a business as a way of surviving because they had to feed their families. They also saw it as a way of creating wealth for themselves. The first Black millionaire was William Leidesdorff, Jr. In 1848, he was San Francisco's wealthiest man, and his land holdings alone were worth at least $1.5 million. That was more than $30 million in today's money.

In addition, in 1800, Mary Ellen Pleasant became one of the first African-American female self-made millionaires. Despite the significant obstacles she faced as a Black woman, Pleasant employed her inherent savvy into building a massive investment portfolio that was reportedly worth as much as $30 million at one time. That fortune would have made her close to a billionaire in today's value. She put her fortune to use by aiding abolitionist causes across the country while helping slaves escape through the Underground Railroad and to settle down in free states (Huddleston, 2020).

Annie Malone, a millionaire with assets of $14 million in 1920, was the owner of Poro College. *Poro* is a West-African word meaning "physical and spiritual growth." Poro College was a five-story facility with a manufacturing plant, a retail store that sold products, a 500-seat auditorium, a rooftop garden, and business offices. The college was for Black women. She wanted women to learn the skill of cosmetology as well as give back to their community. While many people have not heard of her, she is considered the mother of the hair care and cosmetic industry. Her college also employed nearly 2,000 people in St. Louis. Through its school and franchise businesses, her business created nearly 75,000 jobs for women in North and South America, Africa, and the Philippines. Madam C.J. Walker, another millionaire, created the "Walker System," a system used for scalp preparation, application of lotions, and ironing combs. She had the gift of self-promotion with a personal touch, which propelled her business to empire status. She employed more than 3000 workers, mainly salespeople, who sold door-to-door to Black women (Editors H. , 2020). As Black Americans accrued wealth through Black-owned businesses, this was a threat to white-dominated American capitalism.

"In 1906, O.W. Gurley, a wealthy African-American from Arkansas, moved to Tulsa and purchased over 40 acres of land that he made sure was only sold to other African-Americans," writes Christina Montford in the *Atlanta Black Star*. Gurley provided an opportunity for those migrating "from the harsh oppression of Mississippi." The average income of Black families in the area exceeded "what minimum wage is today." As a result of segregation, a "dollar circulated 36 to 100 times" and remained in Greenwood, Oklahoma "almost a year before leaving." This area was called Black Wall Street. Even more impressive, at that time, the "state of Oklahoma had only two airports," and "six black families owned planes" (Fain, 2017). On May 31 of that year, the *Tulsa Tribune* reported that a black man, Dick Rowland, attempted to rape a white woman, Sarah Page. Whites in the area refused to wait for the investigative process to play out, sparking two days of unprecedented racial violence. Thirty-five city blocks went up in flames; 300 people died, and 800 were injured. Defense of white female virtue was the expressed motivation for collective racial violence.

While approaching the 100th anniversary of the destruction of Black Wall Street, there have been several other occurrences when aggression hindered and stopped business growth. For instance, the murder of Elmore Bolling, a successful Black businessman, by his jealous white neighbor in Alabama in 1949, is just a glimpse of the pattern of racist violence that terrorized African-Americans for generations. On a broader scale, White Americans destroyed prosperous Black businesses in many communities (Clegg II, 2018).

While lynching(s) occurred in the past, Black Americans still pushed on to carve out a path of American history. People like Arthur George (A.G.) Gaston was born in a log cabin in Demopolis, Alabama, in 1892, he defied the social climate of the times to become a business leader, and later, a behind-the-scenes political leader at a critical time in civil rights history. He was a multimillionaire by the middle of the 20th century. He ran an insurance company and his funeral home business, Smith and Gaston, had 13 branches in Alabama. He later opened his own savings and loan bank, a business college, and his own motel—the Gaston motel (Smith, 2010).

Reginald F. Lewis, "Reg", as they called him, in 1987, became the first African-American to acquire a billion-dollar business. Oprah Winfrey, Bob Johnson, Michael Jordan, Tyler Perry, and Robert F. Smith all have achieved billionaire status as entrepreneurs. I am not saying that everyone needs to be a billionaire, but there needs to be a concentrated effort to utilize and invest our money to create an economic foundation.

Black America's Buying Power

Since the end of the last economic downturn, African-American buying power has seen impressive gains, jumping from $961 billion in 2010 to an estimated $1.3 trillion in 2018. Since the year 2000, the African-American market has seen a 114 percent increase in buying power. The boost resulted from a surge in black-owned businesses, increased educational attainment, and booming population growth. The percentage of African-Americans who complete college continues to rise (23 percent in 2017, up from 17 percent in 2000).

The population has grown by 22.7 percent since 2000, faster than the national average of 16.3 percent. The African-American population's youthfulness skews the group's buying power downward, as a larger share of the population has yet to hit their peak earning years.

The ten states with the greatest Black buying-power growth since 2000 are North Dakota (1,051 percent); South Dakota (502 percent); Idaho (375 percent); Wyoming (339 percent); Vermont (320 percent); Arizona (265 percent); Montana (255 percent); Maine (243 percent); Utah (235 percent) and New Hampshire (226 percent). All have flourishing African-American consumer markets, but none are among the nation's ten largest Black consumer markets (University, 2019).

While times are not as oppressive as 100 years ago, there are still opportunities for improvement for Black entrepreneurs because, most noted, Black America does not have an impressive economic foundation. Moreover, African-Americans are heavy consumers and not producers. To change the trajectory we must control our destiny, and it is important to broker our causes in this society, especially Black men, as we have the highest unemployment rate in the United States.

Why Black Men Need to Create Their Own by Investing in Stock, Assets, and Businesses

The unemployment rate for Black men is the highest among gender and all racial groups. With that being true, how do we change those figures? Given that we have fought and continue to fight for equality and equal rights, should we as men continue to wait for policies, politicians, and the majority of society to give us what we deserve? Absolutely not! I am not saying to stop advocating and pushing for change; I am saying we must shift our energy into creating for ourselves.

My passion for justice and equality for the Black community is extremely important because if you look at any economically depressed community, you will see a higher concentration of crime and a higher percentage of dilapidated homes. There also is a lack of commerce that is vital to the needs of the community. These communities are also on the short end of the stick for funding and resources from cities and states unless there is a huge project to benefit all the other communities. These communities are deprived by various policies instituted from the past and present, which has a trickle-down effect on citizens' hope. It is true in some parts of our communities, that we as African-Americans need to take more responsibility in maintaining our residences and communities. An immediate solution will be more funding for our communities in housing, business development, and entrepreneurship. There also needs to be more involvement from our churches. I say churches because they are the economic engines of our community. Many Black Americans that live throughout cities still attend church in a Black community. With their financial resources, Black churches could boost Black businesses if they work together collectively. That would boost Black communities and businesses. The churches would play a vital role, however, there are still many needed resources to level the playing field between the majority, and the Black community and Black businesses.

Yes, it is true that the United States government owes Black America reparations, but don't wait on government to give it to you. Start today by creating your own!

When looking at Black communities and businesses, you cannot say that one is progressing better than the other; with both having unequal resources and a lack of an economic foundation. To build this foundation, it takes government assistance and municipal and personal investment of stakeholders. These stakeholders are those that live outside and inside Black communities.

Those that reside in these communities play an important role in its growth and sustainability. A way of taking greater ownership in the community is by ensuring the maintenance and upkeep of properties. Many people speak as if Black communities are run down and crime-infested—their existence—are a Black problem. No. As I see it, the problems in Black communities are not just a Black problem but a poor-community problem that encompasses all communities. For example, I was a project manager in Community Development in Lafayette, Indiana, back in the 1990s. We hired a consultant to discuss strategies for improving neighborhoods. Lafayette, Indiana was easily more than 88 percent White, and some neighborhoods needed a facelift. I remember him coming into the filled meetings with residents to give them strategies for improving their community. At the beginning of the meeting, one of the first statements that came out of his mouth was, "If you want to change your community's look, you need to get the couches off your front porch and clean up around your neighborhood." I agreed with him, as this thought came to me: dilapidated buildings, unkempt yards, and trash in communities are not just a Black problem, they are a *poor* community problem. I say that because often, where you see citizens who do not have adequate economic resources, high unemployment and poverty, the previously mentioned conditions exist.

To change the course of our neighborhoods and economic position, we must take a more deliberate step. This is especially true for Black men, because with the highest unemployment rate among any gender or race, we must look at additional options in life. Moreover, I also am of the notion that if somebody is not going to give you a job, you should create your own. This could be done by investing in stocks, assets, and businesses.

CHAPTER 10: Wealth-Creating Strategies

Before integration, many Black Americans created jobs and opportunities through different income streams, simply because they had to survive. As my mother told me, during those days you either worked or starved. For Black men or for anyone to truly create wealth, they must create different streams of income that lead to financial growth for themselves and their communities. This is not a call to quit your current job; rather, it is a call to begin taking more deliberate steps to create other income streams through investing, acquiring assets, and creating businesses. Various ways of investing exist, including investing your own cash or becoming a part of the operations of a business. You could invest in the stock market, real estate, or a business. Acquiring assets could be in the form of purchasing property, Certificates of Deposit (CDs), Bonds, and Real Estate Investment Trusts (REITs). Another form of investing is through investing in a business. You could either purchase a franchise, or create a business. Below are examples of how the different forms of investments can help in creating wealth.

Creating wealth is not a get-rich-quick scheme; rather, it is a practice that requires faith, discipline, and patience in making strategic moves.

Investing in the Stock Market

Investing in the stock market is an avenue for Black Americans to create wealth. It is a long-term process. The history of the New York Stock Exchange began with the signing of the Buttonwood Agreement by 24 New York City stockbrokers and merchants on May 17, 1792, outside of 68 Wall Street under a Buttonwood tree. The stock market was not only in New York; in 1790 the Philadelphia Stock Exchange, originally named the Board of Brokers of Philadelphia, was founded.

The American Stock Exchange (AMEX) got its start in the 1800s and was known as the "Curb Exchange" because it met as a market at the curbstone on Broad Street near Exchange Place. Its founding date is generally considered to be 1921 because this was the year when it moved into new quarters on Trinity; however, the American Stock Exchange became official in 1953. The National Association of Securities Dealers Automated Quotations (NASDAQ) began trading on February 8, 1971 as the world's first electronic stock market, trading for over 2,500 securities. In November 1998, the American Stock Exchange merged with the National Association of Securities Dealers, creating "The Nasdaq-Amex Market Group." Even so, the American Stock Exchange remained an active exchange (Congress, 2020).

I spoke with Kevin Haggard, Sr., a Certified Financial Planner (CFP), to discuss the importance of investing. He feels there are many of ways of investing, including the stock market. Investing in the stock market helps build wealth without a person being actively involved in the operations of a company. There is no other investment category, over the long-term (10 years or longer), that has given better returns than the stock market. Historically and over the long run, the stock market has returned around 10 percent. The stock market will fluctuate over time, like the mortgage collapse in 2008, when the market tanked. This caused many stocks to lose their value on paper, a value that is subjective and fluctuates on fear, greed, and behavior. For example, the announcement of a Coronavirus vaccine caused the stock market to increase in value. The value on paper is more volatile than the actual value of a company. The actual value consists of its intellectual property, human capital, barriers to entry, equipment, and competitive position. The value of the stock is valued based on the fears or expectations of the market. An advantage of investing in the stock market is that it stays ahead of inflation; your return will be more than inflation. If you are saving, your return is usually less than inflation, which is usually around three percent annually. With investing, the return will be more than inflation. Haggard also believes you need to have a mixture of savings and investing because savings is more accessible, and investing is more long-term and not as accessible.

Haggard feels that Black Americans do not invest because of their lack of investing knowledge. Notably, many are becoming more aware of stocks and are beginning to invest. To get more Black Americans to invest, he feels that we need to utilize existing institutions, such as the church, and educate those in church about stocks and how to invest. In terms of investing, he feels there are some specific priorities:

- Start educating our children about investing and the value of money when they are toddlers.

- Learn the fundamentals of credit and credit management.

- Start the education of personal finance in elementary school.

- Take courses and read books, as you get older, about personal finance and investing.

Investing in Other Assets

Other ways of investing include Certificates of Deposit (CD), Bonds, Real Estate Investment Trusts (REITs), Peer-to-peer lending, and your own product/business. All present various risks, liquidity, and returns on investments.

Certificate of Deposit (CD)

A Certificate of Deposit (CD) is a low-interest investment offered by banks. In essence, you loan the bank money for a set amount of time known as a "term length," and you gain interest on the principal during this time. The term of the CD is typically three months to five years. During this time, you cannot withdraw your money without taking a penalty hit. Certificates of Deposit have been around in some form since the 19th century, and they are at a fixed rate. The rate fluctuates with the market. For example, CDs reached a three-month high in December 1980 and earned 18.65 percent. However, as of April 2020, the return on a CD yielded a .32 annual percentage rate. The drawbacks to CDs are the following:

- **Inflation.** The average inflation rate in the U.S. over the past 60 years is 3.7% — which stands on the high end for most CD interest rates. It means you can *lose money* if you keep your money in CDs owing to inflation.

- **Low aggressiveness**. If you're young, that means you can stand to be much more aggressive with your investments because you have more time to recover from any losses. Your growth potential is much higher. It allows you more wiggle room to invest in riskier assets and potentially earn more money.

- **Length of investment**. You might not be able to go without having your cash for a long time, especially if you have other financial goals for the future (buying a home, vacation, weddings, etc.) (Sethi, 7 best income generating assets to invest in today, 2019).

Bonds

Bonds are like CDs, but instead of lending your money to the bank, you lend it to the government or corporation. The history of bonds dates back to 2400 BC – a stone discovered at Nippur, in Mesopotamia, now present-day Iraq. This particular bond guaranteed the principal's payment of grain, and the surety bond guaranteed reimbursement if the principal failed to make payment (Cummans, 2014). In the United States, bonds became one of the most popular investments when it was introduced in 1935 by Henry Morgenthau, Jr., the then Secretary of the Treasury. The United States has always issued debt, going as far back as the Revolutionary War. When Secretary Morgenthau developed the United States savings bond program, he wanted each savings bond non-marketable. That meant that investors could not sell savings bonds to other investors. Instead, the savings bonds represented a contract between the original purchaser and the United States government. In exchange, the savings bonds would never fluctuate in value. Investors would cash in their savings bonds and receive their original invested principal, plus any interest owed. Combined with the promise that lost savings bonds could be reissued or replaced, the program became instantly popular (Kennon, 2018). There are various bonds to invest in:

- **Government bonds**. The government bond sector is a broad category that includes "sovereign" debt, which is issued and generally backed by a central government.

- **Corporate bonds**. After the government sector, corporate bonds have historically been the largest bond market segment. Corporations borrow money in the bond market to expand operations or fund new business ventures.

- **Emerging market bonds**. Sovereign and corporate bonds issued by developing countries are also known as Emerging Market (EM) bonds. Since the 1990s, the EM asset class has developed and matured to include a wide variety of government and corporate bonds, issued in major external currencies, including the U.S. dollar and the euro, and local currencies (often referred to as emerging local market bonds). Because they come from various countries, which may have different growth prospects, EM bonds can diversify an investment portfolio and provide potentially attractive risk-adjusted returns.

- **Mortgage-backed and asset-backed securities.** Another major area of the global bond market comes from a process known as "securitization," in which the cash flows from various types of loans (mortgage payments, car payments, or credit card payments, for example) are bundled together and resold to investors as bonds. Mortgage-backed securities and asset-backed securities are the largest sectors involving securitization (Investing, 2020).

Real Estate Investment Trusts (REIT)

Real Estate Investment Trusts (REIT) were begun in the 1960s by the United States Congress. The purpose of them was to give people income through the investment of real estate. REITs are like the mutual funds of real estate. It is a collection of properties operated by a company, known as a trust, that uses money from investors to buy and develop real estate. This form of investing is an ideal choice if you want to get involved with real estate investing but do not want to purchase or finance a property. REITs focus on various industries, both domestic and international. You can invest in REITs that build apartments, business buildings, or even healthcare facilities (Sethi, 7 Best Income Generating Assets to Invest in Today - Bond Section, 2019).

Peer-to-Peer Lending

Peer-to-peer (P2P) lending, known as "crowdlending," allows investors to act as banks. You can lend money to a company and later receive a payment with interest. Crowdlending investing can be streamlined and risky, depending on who the crowdfunding company is lending money to. Nonetheless, it could be an investment that could yield higher returns. Given the risks, only invest money you can lose.

Investment Group

Starting an investment group is another way of earning money. You can start this with a group of like-minded individuals who have investment goals, such as purchasing commercial property. It is an excellent way of utilizing your money to earn extra income. For this to work, an investment group needs to be established. You could be a group of individual investors or form a company, such as a limited liability company. In either case, I would advise creating a memorandum of agreement outlining the individual names and scope of the investment goals.

I discussed this concept with a bank executive. He told me that he knew of 12 individuals who contributed $1000 per month over two years. They formed a company, and after two years, they received financing to purchase apartment complexes. From their investment, everyone received a return on their investment. To accomplish this, the collective group required trust, vision, and goals.

Real Estate Investing

Another method of earning income is through real-estate investing. With real-estate investing, one could invest in one property or several. Whatever the case may be, you must have a system in place to minimize your risks to receive a return on your investment. I spoke with Donnie to share his experience with real estate investing and to give further insight into the field.

Donnie got into real-estate investing when he and his wife rented out their house when they moved from Indianapolis, Indiana to North Carolina. They lost money because their tenant could not afford the rent. Looking at the reasons why they lost money forced them to learn about the business of real-estate investing. Through learning more about real estate, he and his wife began to invest more in it. Their investment business has turned into a full-time job for Donnie. He feels the reward for real estate investing is the opportunity to make unlimited income, but the risk is being in situations, such as the pandemic, when tenants might not have income for rent. As he sees it, it is business, and all business has risks. To minimize his risks, he incorporated a business model in making his units look like a place he would like to live in. Therefore, an emphasis is placed on the quality of his units and tenants and not on the quantity.

He feels that it is not easy to get into real estate, because it takes a little bit of education and capital. For example, if one has too much capital and not enough education, one could lose the capital; therefore, he feels there must be a balance. His best practices in operating his company include the following:

- Make sure you treat the company as a business.

- Make sure you put quality tenants in your real estate on the frontend.

- Do not cut corners in your units, e.g., painting rooms a dark color to hide imperfections.

Investing in a Product or Business

There are various ways to create a product or start a business. You can purchase an existing business, such as a franchise, buy part ownership of an existing business, become a partner, or create a business originated by yourself. Starting a business requires much insightful and realistic planning. You have to plan for who will be on your team, how you will run your operations, how you will promote it, who are your competitors, etc. Planning is a continuous process that encompasses looking at your company from different views such as the financial, the spiritual, and the personal perspective, for starters. Financially, you must plan according to your budget, financial resources, and access to capital. You also have to count the costs, which means knowing what you are getting into and understanding what is required to get it. Spiritually, you have to look at what type of culture you want to operate in and establish core values for your company.

While planning and working your business, you will have frustrating days when you ask yourself why you got into it. Operating a business requires a mental, physical, and spiritual approach. It can be stressful. You should ask yourself if you are healthy enough to run it because it is extremely important to counter that stress instead of letting it build up inside and damage your body. I handle my stress by riding my bike. While riding it, I see God's beauty and feel the effects of it. There is a saying that if you fail to plan, you're planning to fail. Regardless of what you deem necessary in arranging or planning, it is a must to plan. To have an effective plan, you must have a vision of your plan and how you plan to carry it out.

Your Vision to Create a Business

Having a vision outlines how you see your business operating and being successful. Often, our vision comes out of our dreams. For example, can you remember dreaming of becoming a millionaire, a superstar, or CEO of a Fortune 500 company? Well, dreaming is a phenomenon that creates imagination, creativity, and ideas. Our dreams can originate from our subconscious thoughts or in our spirit. A dream can occur once or reoccur several times. When the same dream reoccurs, it is a call for action, and it could very well be a blueprint for your vision. By definition, a vision is having the foresight to see what is to be and wishing what could happen in one, two, or three years. Equally important, having the vision also encompasses knowing or having an idea of what resources are needed to accomplish your vision. This is important. The Bible states that without a vision, the people shall perish. I believe that if you do not have a vision, your company could fail because lack of vision opens the sails in the wind to go in any direction. From your vision, there should be a call to action. My call to action was starting a business.

A call to action is an occurrence that continuously prompts your conscience to change and affect a situation. Putting the pieces of a call to action together can be puzzling, so bringing understanding to it requires a spirit of discernment, willpower, and follow-through. Incorporating the below steps can also bring about further clarity:

- **Pray and meditate:** The power of prayer and meditation gives you direction on what you should do, how you should do it, and when to do it.

- **Journal what enters your mind:** Write your thoughts down to have a record of them.

- **Organize your work:** After recording it in your journal, turn it into an action plan of execution, outlining the cost, market, product/service, deliverables, goals, etc.

- **Become a continuous learner:** Researching what has been bestowed upon you and learning the craft, trade, and techniques will elevate your proficiency and efficiency.

- **Seek wise counsel:** Receiving help and advice could give you another perspective that could revolutionize your call to action. This assistance should come from those who are trusted and credible.

Timing and follow-through are essential once you have put the pieces of your business together and have established a foundation. Rudyard Kipling's poem "IF" says, "If you can dream and not make dreams your master," and is very meaningful, because many of our dreams just remain dormant and never become a reality if we don't move on them. Above all, the driving force in making your call to action a reality requires faith, which is "The substance of things hoped for and the evidence of things not seen." (Hebrews 11:1) If you incorporate the above strategies, you will begin planning and mapping out how you want your business to look and where you want it to go. To make your planning more relevant, you should develop a business plan. A business plan outlines the various areas of the business and plans to take in order to operate it. Your business plan not only serves as a document of your thoughts, it also is a guide for you and provides documents to present to banks and possible investors. Below are key components you need to have in your business plan:

Executive Summary

This opening section kick-starts your business plan and briefly outlines the key points of it. The goal here is to explain what your company does and why it will be successful. Include a company mission statement (i.e., your goals for the business, in just a sentence or two).

Business Description

This section leads off the main portion of your business plan. In it you'll go into more detail on what your company does and what solutions it brings to the marketplace. In this section, you need to be specific and detail what products or services you're developing and what customers you're targeting. Include a brief history of your company and mention any top-level talent you have on board to get your company off the ground.

Market Analysis

In this section, you'll detail the marketplace you'll be competing in by outlining a Strength, Weakness, Opportunity, and Threat (SWOT) analysis. Where are the best opportunities in your business, who are your competitors, and what are the company's strengths and weaknesses? Developing a SWOT analysis shows that you are aware of your internal operations and what external challenges or traps exist. In other words, it shows that you know who is leading in your marketplace and what you are doing differently to improve on the leading products or services. Financing companies want to work with differentiators, and they would want to know what separates your business from the pack. Here's the place to tell them precisely that.

Company Organization

How will your company operate (i.e., as a partnership or corporation), and who will be the key decision-makers? How will the company be structured legally? There are different structures for your company: sole proprietorship, general partnership, limited liability company, and corporation. Within the corporation, you can have S corps.

Sole Proprietorship

A sole proprietorship is a business that is owned by a single individual. It is the easiest type of business structure to form because no paperwork is needed to file with the state unless you want to run your business under a name different from your own. Depending on the business, such as a barbershop, you might need a license or permit to operate in that city and state. Sole proprietorship businesses are attractive to many because they are not bogged down with government regulations. They also do not have to deal with owners, boards, or shareholders' oversight, and they report their income on their personal taxes.

A major disadvantage of a sole proprietorship is that you are personally liable for any business-incurred debt as the business owner. If sued, you are personally liable. That means all your assets (home, car, etc.). Also, it can be tough to get a bank loan as a sole proprietor.

Depending on your business type, I would be a little hesitant to operate as a sole proprietor, primarily because of the liability you could incur personally. For instance, I was at a conference, and a millionaire businessman said that once you start making money, people will come after you and proposition you, and I believed him. You want to protect you and your assets.

General Partnership

A general partnership is the same thing as a sole proprietorship, the difference being a sole proprietorship involves only one person and a general partnership involves two or more people. Because of its structure, additional work is needed to divide up the business responsibilities and ownership percentages between both owners. Like the sole proprietorship, no paperwork needs to be filed with the state unless you want to operate under a different name.

The key drawback of a partnership is that you are personally liable for your partners' mistakes. For example, if one of your partners accidentally injures a customer, both of you will be held liable, and that can affect your business and personal assets.

Having a partner can be a win-win situation for both, however, I would advise that each partner's role and details be written in a contractual form and notarized because one never knows the future. For example, a partner could get killed in an accident, leaving the other partner with difficult decisions to make. I have worked with people who developed partnerships with their boyfriend or best friend, which is all good until the relationship or friendship breaks down. You must have a clear understanding of each other's management style and role in the company.

Corporation

A corporation is a business entity recognized as a separate legal entity from its owners, and a corporation is a whole different animal. Corporations are more complicated to set up and are different from sole proprietorships and general partnerships. A corporation has the ability to conduct business, sue, or be sued. One common type of corporation is the S-corporation. Unlike the previous two business structures, there is actual paperwork required for an S-corporation.

An S-corporation, commonly called an S Corp, is a unique corporation under the IRS tax code. Under this system, the profits and losses can pass through to your tax return, and the business is not taxed. Only the owners of the business are taxed and it **protects the corporation from double taxation.**

The owners of a corporation are called shareholders. The primary advantage of having a corporation is the limited liability it grants its shareholders. That means an owner is only liable for the amount he/she has invested in the business. Another benefit of a corporation is it can implement a benefit and profit-sharing program for its employees.

Limited Liability Company (LLC)

The Limited Liability Company (LLC) is a business structure that acts as a corporation but is not one. It is not a corporation, but it can still provide the corporate-like protection that is important for many business owners. An LLC can be taxed as a sole proprietorship, partnership, or S-corporation, and income and expenses can pass through to its members' (owners) individual tax returns.

In all the cases above it is extremely important for you to not mix your personal money with a business and vice versa. How you treat your customers, finances, the activity inside and alongside your business, and even your company's patrons will tell the story about your business. The quality of service customers receive might be their perception, which could be their reality. That is why, being a business owner, you must be consistent in offering a quality service to all customers.

Products or Services Provided

A product is an item that you can physically see that you've made or purchased to sell to a customer. An example would be making a computer to sell to customers. A service is something that is provided by someone or people in an effort to sell to customers. In developing your business plan, you have to ask what will your company produce and how will it benefit customers? Is your product or service a need or want among customers? What kind of research and development have you already put into your company? What results are you getting and expecting? Also, how will you market your product or service to customers? These are the questions you'll need to answer in this section.

Financial Analysis of Your Company

In this section, you will need to lay out your financial projections for your company. If your company is already up and running, list any balance sheets, income statements, and cash flow numbers from the past several years. Do you have any outstanding loans? What are your quarterly projections going forward? Company funders consider this the most important section of your business plan. You must be thorough and as accurate as possible in presenting financial data to potential investors because they'll be pouring over every word and every digit to judge whether it is a good business opportunity or not.

Your company financials are the utmost important aspect of running your business. You cannot trust or let someone else handle your finances without knowing your actual numbers yourself. I have worked with several companies and have witnessed several companies go down because they did not have a good understanding and grip on their finances. Your finances give a clear picture of the direction the company is going in.

Summary

To sell your business plan, have supporting data, graphs, and charts that bolster your pitch. Make it clear what you're looking for financially from financiers—equity, a partnership, or a loan. Provide an estimate of the funding you need, and make it clear whether you're open to negotiation. A company that knows how much money it needs will be taken seriously and treated as such by funders and financiers (O'Connell, 2018).

Developing a Business Model

The beauty of owning a business is you are in total control of how it looks and where it's going. The pleasure to me in being a business owner is the ability to dream and put a vision into action to help people. I found that we often come up with our vision from our experiences, both positive and negative, and we turn those experiences into power. When I say power, I am saying it could be something that could change the community's face or create a need for a customer base. To lay the foundation for your business, you must look at what direction you are going in and forecast where you see it in 5, 10, 15, and 20 years. Some might look at this as a little crazy because we don't know where we're going to be 20 years from now. But we need to think ahead in everything we do regarding our life and business. For example, you might have a transportation and logistics company and plan to own 2,000 autonomous trucks 20 years from now. You also might plan to sell your company to another company in 10 to 15 years. Those are legitimate plans you could put in place, and the sky is the limit with one's planning and investment for their business. So, how do we know if we are making the right business moves in making investments? To safeguard your business, you need to develop a business model to ensure that you get a fair Return on Investment (ROI).

A business model is how you're going to operate your company and the direction it is going, what type of customer you are to serve, what type of services you're going to offer, and the list can go on and on. Your business model derives from your experiences, coupled with your know-how in running and operating a business. While owning and operating a business might be a new venture, I would advise that you seek wise counsel to develop your company's business model. Many services can give you advice, both free and paid, regarding what resources are needed, what direction your company should go, and how it should be grown. I also advise that once you get your business filed with the state, exercise wisdom with whom you do business and from whom you receive wise counsel. When your business is on fire with growth, you're going to have other companies that will solicit your business, claiming to be experts in their field. They are just another company looking to make money from you and give you many false hopes and false dreams. Always do your research on a possible service provider as well as check references.

Many might think a business model is the same as a business plan. It is not. A business plan outlines the operations of a company. A business model outlines how and what way your company will function. A business model describes its position within the industry value chain and how it organizes its relations with potential customers. Having this in place will position your company to maximize revenue and profit. So how do you develop a business model for your company?

For starters, look at what products and services you're going to offer while planning out your company. There are hundreds of companies that sell a product or service, but what would make your product or service unique? Moreover, develop a vision that reflects what you believe in and how you will treat the customer. When developing your company's vision, create a list of what services and products you would like to offer.

Developing your business model for your company will require time, effort, and money. I would carefully think about what products or services to offer. The prices of products and services could be profitable for your company if purchased at a reasonable price and sold to your customers at a profitable margin. Therefore, develop a list of products and services you would like to sell. Determine the cost of those products and services. Determine the price you're going to charge, since this would be a great starting point in planning your business model.

Building Relationships to Grow Your Business

If people think they can grow their business all by themselves they are sadly mistaken. Whether growing your business or moving up the corporate ladder, you need others' help and support. The help could come in several ways. It could come through guidance or someone opening doors so that you may have better access to opportunities.

While completing my master's degree years ago at the University of Louisville, I naively asked an administrator how many doors would open for me now that I had an advanced degree in my pocket. He directly replied and said to me, "I know this is not the answer you are looking for; however, having your master's and not knowing anyone is like having only a quarter in your pocket. It will only get you so far." I was surprised by this statement because we are often told that getting your education opens the doorway of opportunities and success.

As I reflected on our conversation, it became crystal clear to me what he was saying. While education is a necessity, it does not necessarily guarantee success in this competitive society. So, I pondered on the question, how does a Black man create opportunities for himself to become successful in America? Working hard and running three times as fast is a must in this society for a Black man, but having a strategy behind your hard work is key, taking deliberate steps to build and expand your network base. It requires being in the right place at the right time. In addition, creating and promoting a positive personal brand while having faith in God will put you in the right position, at the right time, and in the right place.

A network base is a group of people who might have common interests from whom you might seek advice and possible assistance. Your network is not only Black people or family members, but includes those who have trust and confidence in you, ones you respect and trust. My network carries back more than 25 years, and it comes from people I attended church with, worked with, and volunteered with. Through developing those relationships, doors opened for me as well as for my children.

To expand on your network base, develop relationships with those with shared interests. You can accomplish this through networking, volunteering with business organizations, and conducting informational interviews. Networking is not a one-and-done process. It is continuous. It requires being flexible, and sometimes operating out of your comfort zone. Next, you have to create your brand. Your brand is a marketing term that tells the story of who you are as a person. For instance, your brand might convey that you are a likable, diligent, innovative, and a dependable person. If you have that type of brand, many opportunities will come your way.

Networking, asking the Lord for favor, and having a strong personal brand will put you on the road to accomplishing your goals, but it requires preparation, practice, and follow-through. Below are some tips you should focus on to be successful in networking and establishing your brand:

Pray and ask the Lord for favor in placing the right person and people in your path. This is the most important advice I can give, because God is the true and only Game Changer. He can open doors that appear to be closed and change the minds and hearts of people.

Be true to yourself. Conduct an inventory of who you are as a person. Determine your likes, dislikes, values and goals you want to accomplish. Be comfortable in your skin and know who the woman/man is in the mirror.

Develop a strategy. Evaluate your strengths and weaknesses and do a SWOT analysis to build your business/life plan; then, you will know what/who is needed to assist you in achieving your goals.

Do the work. After developing a strategy to do the work, realize that it will take faith, relationship-building, and a belief you can turn negatives into positives.

Remember the people who helped you become successful. As you become competent in your business, career, and life, remember those who assisted you.

Help others. As you grow by doing the work, spread the seed of helping others. By doing so, you will reap greater returns.

Always reinvent yourself. To sustain your life or business, you must remain innovative by staying abreast of new practices and trends. You can accomplish this through continuous education, reading journals, research, and being a part of think tanks.

If you exemplify through your character and work that you care about your purpose, service, and determination, people and groups will gravitate to you and offer support and advice.

CHAPTER 11: Don't Just Participate in the Political Process; Become a Force Within It

One of the core drivers of the American economy is politics. That is why, for centuries and presently, the right to vote has been denied, highjacked, and undermined. Voting is a right and not a privilege. Even today, the sad reality is that some Americans do not believe that everyone should have that right, or they change the rules so that voting is tilted in their favor. That is because they understand that voting is power. After all, those who represent us can improve the lives of citizens through policies and legislature.

Historically and presently, Black Americans have fought and died for the right to vote. The reason why is white Americans understood the collective power of voting and economic power. To justify their actions, they classified slaves as 3/5 human, then later instituted Jim Crow laws to classify Black Americans as second-class citizens. When you vote, you have a say in what is created, transformed, omitted, and built into a society. Voting is power because you give those representing you the permission to represent and fight for your rights and ideas. As an adjunct professor, I teach my students how important it is to vote. I personally do not understand anyone who does not vote, because it is serious business at every level, whether local, state, or federal. At every level, there is some form of legislation that will directly or indirectly impact you, whether it hits your wallet or your way of life. As I see it, voting is the initial step in becoming actively engaged in the political process.

Presently, the Black community does not vote at the level that it should. Black women vote at a higher level than Black men. Some might argue there are various reasons why that is the case. Nonetheless, I see voting as a precursor for participating in the political process. Not only should the Black community vote, but we must also become more involved in learning, advocating, and demanding policy that impacts our lives. It should not be a reactive but a proactive position.

A policy is a course or principle of action adopted or proposed by a government, party, business, or individual. I was educated in political science and active in community initiatives that involved politics for more than 25 years. Further, there is a great need for African-Americans to become more involved in the political process, especially Black men, by voting and understanding how policies affect us. We need to be able to influence policies that would put the Black community in a better place.

How Can You Change the Political Landscape?

Politicians are voted in by the citizens of cities, states, or nations, and depending on the demographics, it is easier for African-Americans to get into office in areas with larger African-American populations. With that said, should an African-American not run just because there are not enough African-Americans in an area? Absolutely not! I am a firm believer that you must know your constituents, understand their needs, and craft a campaign that includes their needs, and, if elected, deliver on your promises. For example, the late David Dinkins, became the first African-American mayor of New York City from 1990 to 1993, and New York City was easily viewed as a city with various races and ethnic identities.

After graduating from high school in 1945, Dinkins attempted to enlist in the U.S. Marine Corps, but was told that the "Negro quota"

172

had already been met. He eventually was drafted and served in the Marines. He attended Howard University on the G.I. Bill (of Rights), studying mathematics (B.S., 1950). In 1953 he entered Brooklyn Law School and was introduced to politics when he married Joyce Burrows, a New York state assemblyman's daughter. He later joined a law firm and became increasingly involved with the Democratic Party. He was elected to a term in the state assembly in 1965 and later served as president of elections for New York City, as city clerk, and as Manhattan borough president before his successful bid for the mayor's office in 1989. Dinkins took office at a time when New York City was racked by racial discord. Both ethnic tensions and crime statistics increased during his term, and he became the first Black mayor of a major U.S. city to be denied reelection. Dinkins subsequently became a professor at Columbia University (Britannica, 2020).

Today, delivering on your promises is of utmost importance, since your word is your bond. Likewise, I believe there needs to be a change within the current political landscape because some politicians have become too comfortable in their roles. It is easier for them to be re-elected because of name recognition. I also feel that there is need for a change because way too often I've seen politicians take advantage of the African-American community, meaning you only see them coming into the community when they need votes— kissing babies, and passing out food to Black community constituents. Sadly, this has been going on for far too long, and honestly, it's largely been effective. There needs to be more accountability within the African-American community, for example not voting for candidates simply because they are Democrat or Republican. African-Americans may have different needs and wants from other constituents, and politicians just cannot come into the African-American community and assume that everybody's needs are the same. Because of those various needs and wants, I feel there is a greater need for diverse candidates. That is why I'm calling for African-American men to step up and become a part of the political landscape.

Collectively, African-American women are a driving force in shifting the outcome of elections. When they vote in numbers, election results change. I think that is great, and it is something that you have to take notice of. But where are African-American men? If we are the true leaders that we are intended to be and the role models to our families and communities, we must change how we think and step up by becoming more involved in planning and development. How can this happen? It happens by changing how we operate, how we work with each other, and how we see ourselves.

When I say change, I zero in. I asked my students, why do you feel African-American males are good at sports? The answer I received was that we are naturally gifted. That is true to a point. I shared this answer: We spend hours at the playground playing the sports recreationally, and the more we play, the better we become. I juxtaposed the concept of playing sports recreationally for hours to studying coursework for hours at a time. The results would be the same, meaning, the more time we put into our studies, the better we become at that subject matter. To get politics into our African-American young men's minds, we have to start the conversation about politics early and show them its effects by having discussions in our households. How do we create a paradigm shift to getting more African-Americans, particularly men, involved in the political process? Below are my thoughts on harvesting more involvement in politics:

Create a legislative strategic plan for your community. A legislative strategic plan consists of assessing what is happening within a community and developing plans of where the constituents would like to see the community improve, and what type of representatives they want in the future. It consists of determining what projects are needed, their costs, and what type of human capital is required.

Have conversations about politics and the community in your barbershops, jails, churches, and schools. This approach works. When I was a little boy, my father would take me to get my hair cut, and he and his barber would talk about everything that was happening in the community and politics. As an interested young man, I would always listen intently just to hear what they were discussing.

Create legislative clubs. Legislative clubs will teach and mentor young men and women about the political process. This type of organization should teach the beliefs and practices of all political parties.

Develop Political Action Committees (PAC). A PAC is an organization that collects money to distribute to candidates who support the same issues as the contributors. It is a money payment or other form of aid that the government gives to a person or organization.

Being ingrained in the political process is necessary for the Black man if he is seeking to change his own life and community. Given what has happened to African-American males historically and presently, now is the time to develop solutions in this society. There has been an increase in the number of African-American legislators, but there is a need for more. It is up to us to go after them. Let's do it.

CHAPTER 12: Where Do We Go From Here?

The United States is a capitalist society and money drives policies and behavior. That is why slavery came into place and existed in the United States to build the economic foundation of this country. Slavery was not just a money-making venture solely in the South. The North played a role in financing the transport of enslaved persons. Because economics control this country, some still attempt to keep Black Americans in that place of economic bondage. If you're going to keep someone from having any power or true freedom, you deprive them by taking away access to economic resources.

When we look at society, Black Americans have to look at why we are in our position. We have to tell the facts, and the fact of the matter is that racism impacts Black Americans. Since slavery policies and laws have been put into place that disenfranchised and hindered Black Americans from progressing at the same rate as their white counterparts. Black Americans were prevented and cheated from using the GI bill, cheated from purchasing homes, and cheated by welfare programs that dissuaded women from marrying men. The three-strikes program exacerbated the incarceration rate of Black and brown people. All those policies and laws contributed to the breakdown of economic progress of Black America, all of which have been consequential in the Black community, and impacted all families and the breakdown of those communities. I am not making any excuse for anyone who commits a crime, but statistics show that the probability of crime increases when there is a lack of economic opportunities. For instance, The United Nations reported a consistent relationship between specific crimes and specific economic factors. The evidence shows that crime is linked to the economic climate. Such findings are consistent with the criminal motivation theory, which suggests that economic stress increases criminal behavior. "The presence of youth gangs, the availability of weapons and potential targets, drug, and alcohol consumption, and the effectiveness of law enforcement all play a significant role in enabling or restraining overall crime levels (United Nations Office of Drugs and Crime, 2012). You can easily trace that many of those involved in crime came from homes that were broken, having negative role models, economic deprivation, and social isolation. The economic and social ills have persisted into 2020 and could be a breaking point in America.

The year 2020 further highlighted and complicated race relations, police relations, and equality in the United States. There was the fatal shooting video of Ahmaud Arbery that was viewed by most Americans. Breonna Taylor, a Black medical worker, was shot and killed by Louisville, Kentucky police officers in March during a botched raid at her apartment. Led by wide-scale demonstrations, the cases drew national and global attention. Moreover, the killing of George Floyd blew open the outcry of injustice in America. What made matters worse was when Kentucky Attorney General Daniel Cameron did not charge the three police officers who fired shots into Breonna Taylor's apartment. The incidences of police brutality are a continuation of a systemic problem here in the United States. Several people, notably Colin Kaepernick, have raised a voice to the problem, only to be overlooked, or for the media to twist their motives in saying they are unpatriotic for taking a knee. The blatant injustices have left many angry and bewildered, and many have asked what is next and what we can do about it?

Society is forever changing in terms of the diversity of people, expansion of businesses, and overall societal structure. Society is also moving rapidly, and if you do not have a plan for keeping pace, you could be left behind. Sadly, we are in the United States, and it appears that there are factions that want to turn back the hands of time for

African-Americans and other minorities. They are trying to change the hands of time through policies and other tactics to disenfranchise and divide people. That is why it is essential to exercise your power to vote and to get involved in the political process. Some believe that voting does not matter, but I ask them, if it did not matter, why are great efforts put into stopping people from voting and why is there redistricting so that votes can be swayed toward a political party?

Regardless of what is going on in society, there are elements that we cannot control, and things that we can control. What we can control are our actions. That is why we need to begin today to map out our course as Black men. We must look into the mirror and be true to ourselves and correct what is wrong in our lives. We also must change and control our narrative and the direction we are collectively going in. We must do the following:

- Trust that God will protect, lead, and guide us.

- Be committed to respecting ourselves, our fellow man, our significant other, and our community.

- Be committed to creating wealth for ourselves, and build an economic foundation for our community.

- Man up and don't let racism hold us down, and treat racism as a hurdle to jump over.

- Be true to ourselves and clean up what we messed up, whether that is a relationship with our significant other or failing to be the father we ought to be to our children.

- Strive to be leaders in our families, communities, churches, corporate America, politics, and entrepreneurship.

- Do the right thing always and keep going forward at all costs!

The key to us progressing as Black men depends on our respect for one another and collectively capitalizing on our abilities. We can do it, and I have faith that we will keep going, no matter what!

CHAPTER 13: Keep Going Forward at All Cost! A Strategy for Executing and Sustaining Your Business

I am a man who always thirsts for knowledge. I am also an optimist and a believer that my success depends on my faith, attitude, and drive, no matter what this society throws at me. I know I can because of the accomplishments Black men who came before me achieved during very oppressive times. For example, I look at the Tuskegee Airmen and what they accomplished. They faced constant, overt discrimination throughout their time serving the United States Air Corps during World War II, and they still marched on, excelling above the rest. I see the Olympic champion Jesse Owens, who faced discrimination, and he still ran on. I see Reginald F. Lewis, who fought through many barriers to become the first Black man to acquire a billion-dollar company and whose mantra was to, "Keep Going No Matter What!" I see my father, who started cleaning up in a brace shop in 1957, and later going back to school to get his education and certification then, in 1977, becoming the Director of Orthotics and Prosthetics. I see former Atlanta mayor Maynard Jackson, who opened the door for prosperity for many African-American entrepreneurs in Atlanta. I see our brother's keeper, Marion Barry, who opened many doors for African-Americans in Washington, D.C. These are just a few people who fought through adversity and still made it to their professions' pinnacle. Seeing these men fight through barriers, I say to myself, if these men still excelled within their area of expertise during those more oppressive times, why can't I? They give me hope and motivation in knowing whatever I want to achieve I can do it if I put the work into it and have faith.

As you journey through life, you will find the cards could be stacked against you and that certain people may be against you. The reality is not everyone is going to be for you. You cannot focus on who is not for you, because not everyone can see, or even support your dream. That is what I told my son Hilton. This society does not care about your success or not. That's why it is totally up to you to succeed. With God by your side, the cards will be in your favor. Below are some steps I use to reassure and secure my faith and focus in my life journey. It is my prayer that these action steps support you.

- **Always Put God first and Go After Your Goals with Faith and Focus.** We all dream of a better life, and sometimes we do not know how to transform our dreams into action steps. To bring our dreams into reality, we have to put goals and steps in place. When putting those goals in place, it sometimes scares us into thinking it is not achievable. Regardless of where you are, your dreams can become a reality if you have faith, focus, and are not be afraid to move forward with them. I recall Bishop Bonner, pastor of Word of Faith Cathedral in Austell, Georgia, say, "If your dreams do not scare you, they are not large enough. You have to take that leap in faith!"

- **Pray the Prayer of Jabez Every Day.** In the book of Chronicles, Chapter 4:10 Jabez cried out to the God of Israel, "Oh, that you would bless me and enlarge my territory! Let your hand be with me and keep me from harm so that I will be free from pain." And God granted his request.

- **Keep Your Eyes on the Prize.** You should focus on the direction you seek to go, having the goal in mind. If you focus on what's going on in society, you could risk being distracted from staying on your path to success. For example, if you drive your car and focus on your rear-view mirror, you could swerve and get off course because you are not focusing on what is in front of you.

- **Be Careful Who You Share Your Ideas With.** I believe it is imperative to seek wise counsel. Wise counsel can give you sound advice on the direction you're going in life as well as hold you accountable. With that said, you cannot share all of your ideas, thoughts, and passion with just anyone because everyone is not your friend. Some people are only in your corner to profit from you. The way to determine if you should share your ideas with a person depends on your relationship's quality, longevity, and what your spirit tells you. If their actions show a consistent pattern of being truthful, that could be a person you could trust. But even in that case, you still should not show your entire hand.

- **Surround Yourself with Like-Minded People.** The power of relationships can either propel or sink you, and the truth of the matter is, the company that you keep is a reflection of who you are as a person. It makes a clear statement of your character where you possibly could be going. Thus, work to position yourself around people who are going in the same direction. It is essential because those relationships could serve as a sounding board and a support system which could lead to further opportunities. Expanding your base of being around like-minded people does not mean you should dismiss your existing family or friends, because in life you will find that all of us have different abilities, and each person brings certain values and attributes.

- **Do Not Be Afraid to Fail.** My sister Stephanie and I talk several times a week. Those discussions are often spiritual as well as empowering. She can hold her own and has never been afraid to step out on faith. She has said several times that she was not afraid to fail but afraid of not trying. That digs deep into my spirit because if something is constantly on your heart and mind, there is a good chance you are supposed to follow through with it.

- **Take Your Failures as Learning Cues.** As you go through life, you're going to have peaks and valleys, great days and disappointing days. I have often said that if you live long

183

enough, you should have a story to tell because life accumulates events that either build us up or tear us down. I have had disappointments as it relates to my profession, relationships, and life. As I see it, disappointments are learning moments. For example, I divorced several years ago, and when it happened, I was embarrassed and angry. Looking at what occurred, I can honestly say that I am a much better man because I had to own up to my own mistakes and reestablish my core principles for relationships. No matter what your failures are in life, keep going forward.

- **Develop and Practice the Spirit of Discernment in All You Do.** We all make mistakes, and I am a firm believer that some mistakes are learning moments and others detrimental. In the learning moments, we must learn, or else we will continue to make the same mistakes over and over and over. We are only human, but before we fall into the land of mistakes we must incorporate the spirit of discernment into our lives. The spirit of discernment is Spirit-driven, giving you pause or permission—impressions (emotional, physical, etc.) that allow you to proceed with what you are doing. To discern what is right and wrong starts with your moral compass, and your spiritual relationship with God.

- **After Receiving Spiritual Confirmation, Be Prepared to Do the Work.** To accomplish anything, you must put work into it. I recently read that success does not happen by occasionally doing the work, but by constantly doing it. That is so true in order to be focused on the goal. That doesn't mean that you won't have any failures. For example, Reginald F. Lewis acquired several companies that were not as successful as his billion-dollar acquisition. Still, he studied and learned from his missteps to better position himself to go after his goals. He did not stop; he kept going, no matter what!

- **Recognize the Terrain You Are Operating On.** While I was president of the National Black MBA Association, Inc. – Kentucky Chapter, I had the opportunity to mentor and provide advice to its members. Members of the organization often stated that opportunities for Black Americans were limited in Kentucky. Moreover, school counselors advised me to leave Kentucky because the MBA was not in demand in Kentucky. When members would talk to me about how they felt being limited by staying in Kentucky, I would always say they might need to move elsewhere to gain that level of success they were seeking. I would explain that success might be on the West Coast, and for others, the East Coast. No matter where you go, what is most important is having the spirit of discernment in knowing the right time and place to go. Wherever you go, understand the terrain and culture you are operating in and adjust your strategy accordingly.

- **Keep Going Forward.** I am a firm believer that learning through adversity fosters success. It allows you to redo or repair what is needed to continue your mission. What am I saying? I am saying you will face hard times, but you cannot let those hard times conquer you. You will have some setbacks, but you cannot let those setbacks distract you. You must continue to march in faith and with focus, and Keep Going Forward, at All Costs!

ABOUT THE AUTHOR

Alan D. Benson is the Founder and President of Benson Group, LLC. He has more than 25 years of experience in leadership roles. He has empowered and managed teams to achieve company goals, created personal and professional growth plans for employees, facilitated training, and created systems that streamlined operations.

Alan is experienced and passionate about helping others reach their true potential, live a purposeful life, and pursue their educational goals. He is a former Advisory Board Member of the University of Louisville College of Business Ulmer Career Center and currently serves as a Board Member of the Metropolitan Business Development Corporation (METCO) and an Adjunct Professor at Simmons College of Kentucky.

Alan believes what we experience in life helps shape our identity, attitude and belief system. From those experiences, he feels it is essential to recognize, decipher, and transform them into actionable steps to achieve our purpose in life. This belief is his driving force in Benson Group, LLC's goal of equipping individuals and companies to reach their true potential.

Alan earned a Bachelor of Science degree in Political Science and a Master of Public Administration degree from the University of Louisville. He also earned a Master of Business Administration degree from Indiana University Southeast. Alan served in the United States Marine Corps and is a Persian Gulf War veteran. He is married to Dr. Debbie Benson and has a stepson, Landon, and twins, Hilton and Hayley.

www.alandbenson.com

BIBLIOGRAPHY

A Brief History of the Drug War. (2020, December 24). Retrieved from Drug Policy Alliance Headquarters: https://drugpolicy.org/issues/brief-history-drug-war

Alliance, D. P. (2020, September 24). *A Brief History of the Drug War.* Retrieved from Drug Policy Alliance: https://www.drugpolicy.org/issues/brief-history-drug-war

America, C. C. (n.d.). 2010 annual report on form 10-K. In C. C. America.

Booker, M. (2016, May 5). *20 years is enough: Time to repeal the Prison Litigation Reform Act.* Retrieved from Prision Policy Initiative : https://www.prisonpolicy.org/blog/2016/05/05/20years_plra/

Britannica, T. E. (2020, November 24). *David Dinkins American Politician .* Retrieved from Britannica: https://www.britannica.com/biography/David-Dinkins

Bunn, C. (2019, December 11). *Blacks in corporate America still largely invisible, study finds.* Retrieved from NBC News: https://www.nbcnews.com/news/nbcblk/blacks-corporate-america-still-largely-invisible-study-finds-n1098981

Clegg II, L. H. (2018, April 28). *Readers React: How lynching was used by whites to destroy competition from black business owners.* Retrieved from Los Angeles Times Newspaper: https://www.latimes.com/opinion/readersreact/la-ol-le-lynching-memorial-business-20180428-story.html

Congress, L. O. (2020, November 24). *Wall Street and the Stock Exchanges: Historical Resources.* Retrieved from Library of

Congress: https://guides.loc.gov/wall-street-history/exchanges

Cummans, J. (2014, October 1). *A Brief History of Bond Investing.* Retrieved from bondfunds.com: http://bondfunds.com/education/a-brief-history-of-bond-investing/#:~:text=The%20first%20recorded%20bond%20in,principal%20failed%20to%20make%20payment.

Editors, H. (2020, June 23). *Civil Rights Movements.* Retrieved from History.com: https://www.history.com/topics/black-history/civil-rights-movement

Editors, H. (2020, March 2). *Madam C. J. Walker.* Retrieved from History.com: https://www.history.com/topics/black-history/madame-c-j-walker

Fain, K. (2017, July 5). Retrieved from JSTOR Daily: https://daily.jstor.org/the-devastation-of-black-wall-street/

Ferris State University, F. S. (2020, September 23). *JIM CROW MUSEUM TIMELINE, PART 2 (1619 - 1865.* Retrieved from Jim Crow Museum: https://www.ferris.edu/htmls/news/jimcrow/timeline/slavery.htm

Gooding, F. (2018). American Dream Deferred: Black Federal Workers in Washington, D.C, 1941 - 1981. In F. Gooding, *American Dream Deferred: Black Federal Workers in Washington, D.C, 1941 - 1981* (p. 347).

Gotsch, K. A. (2018, August 2). *The Sentencing Project .* Retrieved from Capitalizing on Mass Incarceration: U.S. Growth in Private Prisons: https://www.sentencingproject.org/publications/capitalizing-on-mass-incarceration-u-s-growth-in-private-prisons/

Huddleston, J. T. (2020, February 15). *Mary Ellen Pleasant, one of the first black self-made millionaires, used an ingenious trick to build her fortune.* Retrieved from Make it:

https://www.cnbc.com/2020/02/14/how-mary-ellen-pleasant-became-one-of-the-first-black-millionaires.html

Investing, U. (2020, November 28). *Everything You Need to Know About Bonds*. Retrieved from Pimco: https://www.pimco.com/en-us/resources/education/everything-you-need-to-know-about-bonds/

Kennon, J. (2018, December 10). *The History of US Savings Bonds*. Retrieved from the balance : https://www.thebalance.com/the-history-of-us-savings-bonds-358068

Kimbro, P. D. (2020, November 16). *Good Reads*. Retrieved from Good Reads: https://www.goodreads.com/author/quotes/8440.Dennis_Kimbro

Little, B. (2018, October 2). *Does an Exception Clause in the 13th Amendment Still Permit Slavery?* Retrieved from History.com: https://www.history.com/news/13th-amendment-slavery-loophole-jim-crow-prisons

LoBianco, T. (2016, March 24). *Report: Aide says Nixon's war on drugs targeted blacks, hippies*. Retrieved from CNN: https://www.cnn.com/2016/03/23/politics/john-ehrlichman-richard-nixon-drug-war-blacks-hippie/index.html

Lopez, G. (2017, January 19). *How Obama quietly reshaped America's war on drugs*. Retrieved from Vox : https://www.vox.com/identities/2016/12/19/13903532/obama-war-on-drugs-legacy

NAACP. (2020, September 26). *CRIMINAL JUSTICE FACT SHEET*. Retrieved from NAACP: https://www.naacp.org/criminal-justice-fact-sheet/

O'Connell, B. (2018, August 3). *How to Write a Business Plan in Seven Steps*. Retrieved from The Street:

https://www.thestreet.com/how-to/write-a-business-plan-14666639

Sessions, J. (2017, February 21). *Rescission of Memorandum on Use of Private Prisons*. Retrieved from Office of the Attorney General: https://www.bop.gov/resources/news/pdfs/20170224_doj_memo.pdf

Sethi, R. (2019, October 8). *7 best income generating assets to invest in today*. Retrieved from I will teach you to be rich: https://www.iwillteachyoutoberich.com/blog/income-producing-assets/

Sethi, R. (2019, October 8). *7 Best Income Generating Assets to Invest in Today - Bond Section*. Retrieved from I WIll teach you to be rich: https://www.iwillteachyoutoberich.com/blog/income-producing-assets/

Smith, S. E. (2010, December 21). *National Public Radio* . Retrieved from NPA: https://www.npr.org/2010/12/21/132089160/a-g-gaston-from-log-cabin-to-funeral-home-mogul

U. O. (2019, March 21). *Minority Markets Have $3.9 Trillion Buying Power*. Retrieved from Minority Markets Have $3.9 Trillion Buying Power: https://www.newswise.com/articles/minority-markets-have-3-9-trillion-buying-power

United Nations Office of Drugs and Crime. (2012, February 3). *Economic crises may trigger rise in crime*. Retrieved from United Nations Office of Drugs and Crime: https://www.unodc.org/unodc/en/frontpage/2012/February/economic-crises-can-trigger-rise-in-crime.html

United States House of Representative History, A. a. (2020, September 23). *The Civil Rights Movement And The Second Reconstruction, 1945—1968*. Retrieved from United States

House of Representative History, Arts, and Archives :
https://history.house.gov/Exhibitions-and-
Publications/BAIC/Historical-Essays/Keeping-the-
Faith/Civil-Rights-Movement/

Williams, C. (2019, January 26).
https://apnews.com/article/55792de5cc4946b1844c028469389c9
f. Retrieved from AP News:
https://apnews.com/article/55792de5cc4946b1844c02846
9389c9f

Made in the USA
Columbia, SC
09 September 2022

66481108R00107